Dreamlands

Dreamlands

Extraterrestrial Activity
In The Old Testament

Vol. I

Robin Ward

To order additional copies of this book, contact:
Xlibris
1-888-795-4274
www.Xlibris.com
Orders@Xlibris.com
672705

Special thanks to:

Emily Puccini BA
Shirley Ward BA
Lorri Schuetz R.E.C.E. Montessori

Best Wishes

Robin

JN. 3:16 KJV

FOREWORD

IN 1942, I watched as the Battle of Britain unfolded in the skies over London. Then came the Blitz. I witnessed the V-1 and V-2 bombs drop, with their indiscriminate destruction. I also witnessed the dogfights. Sometimes the enemy's plane was the loser, sometimes ours.

Sometime later, I read about eyewitness accounts of Hurricanes and Spitfires continuing to fight after it was obvious that the pilot had perished and was no longer in control of his plane. Sometimes the planes' canopies were blown away, or the aircraft were continuing the battle long after they had expended their quota of ammunition. I personally spoke to one pilot, who was a guest in my home, of just such events. These men have since passed away, but who are we to question eyewitness accounts, or the fact that Hitler ultimately lost these air battles?

These events caused me to begin thinking about extraterrestrials from an early age. The purpose of this book is to discuss extraterrestrial events as described in the Bible from Genesis to Malachi. Some of these events are miracles, and some cannot be explained; but some of them have plausible explanations. I have chosen to use the Received Texts of the Old Testament, originating in Antioch, for the simple reason that all texts from Alexandria have been drastically altered. The best possible texts must be used in order to eliminate the excuse to question the events being covered. I have done my best to cover all the extraterrestrial events in the Old Testament, but if you, the reader, find that I have missed any, please write to me. The omissions will be included in any future reprint.

INTRODUCTION

U FO THEORIES, EXTRATERRESTRIAL theories, other-dimension theories, ancient astronaut theories, ghost theories, and many other theories are filling the airwaves. Mankind has forever been fascinated with the possibility of life outside our universe. Evidence shows that we are being watched. Sometimes the "extraterrestrials" appear in varying forms and scare the pants off most of us. Every television show that I have seen so far links the unknown with evolution in some way, in particular with the Darwinian idea that humanity is on a continuing "upward" progression. Eventually, it has been surmised, we will become part machines or part (or wholly) "spirit" beings.

As far as I am aware, the Bible has not been examined by any commentator dealing only with references to extraterrestrial activity. Most "experts" on the Bible write it off as a book of allegories, philosophical theories, or old wives' tales. In reality, the Bible is not one book, but a compilation of sixty-six different books written over a period of approximately one thousand years, by at least forty different individuals. Most of these writers, or authors, wrote *history*. Others told of the human condition, both glorious and depraved. All the stories and histories relate a no-holds-barred account of the people involved.

The Bible relates the true account of how this system or realm came to be. Archaeology and science have proven the history in the Bible to be true. You may disagree; you are at liberty to form your own opinions. The point of this volume is not to shape your opinion in this regard, but to recount references to extraterrestrials in the first thirty-nine books of the Bible, collectively known as the Old Testament.

Most of us agree that "there is something out there." Can we determine what that "something" is based on the Bible? Any biblical account of extraterrestrial or angelic beings that aid mankind describes these beings as similar to humans in appearance. No bug-eyed reptilians here, and nothing gray, green, or yellow. For what it's worth, the idea of extraterrestrials being "reptilian" always seems to work to man's detriment; we will see why later.

CHAPTER 1

A LL SCRIPTURE WAS written by holy men being moved and inspired directly by Jehovah God through his Spirit. This being true, then Jehovah God wrote the scriptures (indirectly). The original velum and papyrus texts are no longer extant, but we do have correct copies, and copies of copies. Scribes copying the scriptures needed to exactly match their transcription to the original. These scribes were aided in the endeavor by cantors. Cantors may not have been able to read the language of the texts, but they could count the number of letters per line and page. If the cantor spotted any errors, the scribe was compelled to begin the copy over from the beginning. So what we have in our Received Text bibles today is God's Word, kept as accurately as possible.

When Isaiah says that a "virgin" will bear a son, this does not mean that a "young girl" or a "maiden" will bear a son, as many corrupt texts incorrectly state. What follows is a compilation of every extraterrestrial occurrence listed in God's Word. Since it was he who wrote it, why not accept the fact that the Creator can and does break into his creation wherever and whenever he wants? We call some of these occurrences miracles. God's ways are as far above our ways as our ways are above the ants'. God has also said that our imagination cannot begin to comprehend what he has in store for those who love him. He tells us that there is life after death and that we can look forward to this life sometime in the future.

Genesis 1 begins by saying that "in the beginning" (1:1) God created space and matter. The first mention of anything created was this planet; the sun, moon, stars, animals, plants, and mankind were all to come later in the creation week. Jehovah God mentioned here is two persons. Christ's involvement in Creation comes just a little later in the process.

This activity on the part of a being who is able to create is the first mention of extraterrestrial activity in our known universe. The text goes on to say that the Spirit of God moved on the waters. The light was made, then the waters were "divided," some "under" and some "above," with a space in between for the birds to fly. The waters "under" this space are understood to be oceans, lakes, and rivers. The waters "above" the space require some explanation. One possibility is that they were vaporized water such as mist, clouds, or smog. This is unlikely, however, because visibility is negated by mist or clouds. Just try driving through a pea-souper. Mist would also not be able to prevent the earth's heat from escaping. Since it is a proven fact of science that the earth once had a worldwide uniform temperature, there must have been something preventing its heat from escaping. It is most likely that this was an ice canopy, water in its solid form surrounding the earth.

A little later in the texts we read of a forty-day deluge. The only way that this could have happened is for the ice canopy to have melted. My personal conjecture is that this ice canopy closed the earth in like a terrarium, similar to the one we had in public schools, self-contained and self-sufficient. The canopy would have needed to be twenty- to thirty-foot thick to produce forty days and nights of rain as it melted. Its structural integrity likely failed during that melting, and chunks of ice came crashing down. To this day, we have evidence of such ice at the earth's poles. The canopy melt caused a flood of worldwide proportions. All known land was covered to a depth of more than fifteen feet. This event can be read about in Genesis 6.

To return to Genesis 1, verse 3 records that God said, "Let there be light" (not to be confused with verse 14, where he makes "lights" in the sky). This light is a combination of the known spectrum that humans see, ultraviolet light (which most birds can see), x-rays, microwaves, black light, and other types of electromagnetic radiation. On the second day, God made a firmament between the waters, in which the birds fly, and on the third day he brought forth the dry land, followed by plants. The next creation act has always astounded me personally: God made the heavenly bodies on the fourth day. It was only after this that God made fish, animals, and birds.

Keep in mind that the creation days were all only twenty-four-hour periods. A day, as named in the Bible, is only and is always twenty-four hours, all the way from Genesis 1 to Revelation 22. If you don't think this creator God has the ability to do all that work in the time he states, then your God is way too small.

After creating the plants, the heavenly bodies, and all the animals, God made mankind, and all the trouble started.

During Creation, God took a personal, hands-on approach to his work. He became a personality who interacted with the creation. God was an extraterrestrial taking an active part with the animals and, in particular, with Adam and Eve. In Genesis 1 and Genesis 2:1–3, we see the making of our known universe.

Having lived through the Battle of Britain and the Blitz, I can honestly say that I wouldn't wish it on my worst enemy. My grandparents told me stories about the invention of bombs during World War I and how aircraft pilots dropped them by hand, one at a time. At first, these bombs had the ability to knock out a vehicle; soon, the larger ones could knock out a house. Before long, bombs had developed to the point that they could take out a large building, then a city block. By the end of World War II, they could destroy a whole city.

The point is, the bigger the bomb, the greater the destruction. No explosion that either my grandparents or I ever saw had any creative effect on anything. No bomb exploding in a printing factory ever produced an encyclopedia. On the other hand, the explosion of a comet over the Sahara Desert in Egypt did "create" some exquisite green glass.

God's final creative act "in the beginning" was to make mankind. Man is the only created being made in God's image. God is Father, Son, and Holy Spirit, whereas man is body (*soma*), spirit (*ruach-nephesh*), and soul (psyche). It is important to note Genesis 2:21, wherein God, the extraterrestrial, takes some genetic material from man, namely a rib, and uses it to make a female of the species. This does not happen with any other animal, bird, or fish.

Chapter 3 starts out with a talking serpent. Some have made good arguments for a likeness to a dragon in this serpent, such as those pictured in the Rupert books or in Chinese art, and who is to say that this analogy is incorrect? Others believe that the story of the talking serpent is only a figment of someone's overactive imagination, but since God wrote the story, who can make a case against it?

In my opinion, we now have another extraterrestrial coming on the scene. The account of Lucifer being expelled from heaven can be read in Isaiah 14. Isaiah also mentions a dragon and the dimensions of heaven and hell, but more on that later. In Genesis 3, we find two opposing ideologies: that of God the Creator and that of Lucifer, or Satan, the destroyer. At this point, it's difficult not to get involved with Dante. Suffice it to say, one extraterrestrial uses cunning and deception against another extraterrestrial. The winner and the loser of this conflict have already been determined, but the Bible has a lot more to say about extraterrestrial activity on earth throughout the planet's history. All we have to do is to recognize these events and understand how they affect us.

In Genesis 3, Eve listens to Lucifer and succumbs to his temptation. She then seduces Adam, and he also falls into sin, after which God curses the earth and multiplies Eve's sorrows.

I have always found it amazing that even God's curses can be beautiful. Just look at a sunset or at the Rocky Mountains in winter. Marvel at the multiplicity of life in a coral reef or at flocks of migrating birds and butterflies.

To return to Genesis 3, we now read about another type of extraterrestrial, an angel. The cherubim, as far as I can determine, are one rank above the archangels. Above the archangels are the seraphim, followed by God's "bodyguards," the four creatures attending his throne. The lowest-ranking angels are the messenger angels of the type that appear in Zechariah 5, and of which there are both males and females. The cherub guarding the tree of life in Genesis 3:24 holds a flaming sword. Was this a literal sword, or could it have been a laser or even a *Star Trek*–style phaser? I believe that it could possibly have been an even more advanced weapon intended to keep Satan and his gang away from Eden along with Adam and Eve. After all, if Satan exploited the tree of the knowledge of good and evil, why would he not also try to exploit the tree of life?

Genesis 4–6 describes the history of men before the flood. Where was Satan during this time? In hell? No, not yet. The evidence in the record does not say so. In fact, the text tells of a race who knew mining, refining, tanning, metallurgy, and rock carving. We'll discuss the preflood cities soon.

It is in this same passage that we read the not-so-boring genealogies of man from Adam to Noah and that we learn the two reasons why God brought about a worldwide flood. The first reason was that man was inherently wicked and evil of his own accord. The second reason was that Satan and his gang genetically corrupted mankind. Genesis 6 is very clear about this. Theologians generally agree that the so-called sons of God mentioned in 6:2 were fallen angels. The biblical diction is genteel in this passage, but of course, when it states that the sons of God took wives from among the human females, it means that they had intercourse with them and produced offspring. Since the Bible also mentions female angels, we must assume that some of these rebellious creatures were female and that they seduced earth men.

The resulting offspring were not genetically pure humans, like the ones God had created. All in all, these mutants did nothing to make a better world; quite the opposite. God decided to put an end to it.

It seems that Noah and his family were the only group of people with a pure genetic makeup. However, even a good man like Noah did not build the ark alone, any more than Timothy Eaton built the Eaton Centre. In our discussion of the great vessel, we must consult the instruction book for accuracy.

CHAPTER 2

THE BUILDING OF the ark was a colossal project. It was big enough to hold dinosaurs as well as all the other earthbound creatures in their twos and sevens. Recently, a televised debate was held between Ken Ham of the Creation Institute and Bill Nye, "the Science Guy." Although most of Mr. Nye's argumentation lacked merit, he made a sensible observation about the ark's construction, namely, that a structure of such scale made of wooden planks would quickly come apart at the seams.

Since I have a background building log houses out of square logs with chamfered corners, I agreed with Nye's observation. There are ways of cutting logs and putting them together without sawing them into planks, only to be pegged or nailed together. I was also a harness maker before retiring, and any one of the horses I owned could have broken a two-by-ten-inch plank with one kick. Can you imagine the damage a dinosaur could do while getting comfortable in its stall? Sorry, Mr. Ham, but planks won't do the job here; square logs with pitch or caulking would be a better solution.

Museums around the world have bones. Boy, do they have bones. Among them are "human" bones of large size and many miscellaneous skulls of long, supposedly misshapen heads. Genesis 6 explains how they came to be. "There were giants in the earth" (6:4) before the flood, the genetically mutant offspring of the fallen angels. Only eight "genetically pure" humans boarded this big boat. It was large enough for the purpose.

As a harness maker and horse breeder, you get to notice things about the animals that are not immediately obvious to most people; when winter comes, for example, horses grow a thick layer of extra hair. However, everybody knows that many animals hibernate through the winter. It is likely that many animals were also hibernating on the ark.

When the ice canopy collapsed, the earth was no longer uniform in temperature. This sudden inrush of cold air must have made a lot of animals go to sleep. An animal's digestive system slows down while the animal is hibernating, so Noah and his family would not need to shovel out the ark's stalls as often as one might assume. Still, there could have been no open fires for cooking on the lower decks due to the prevalence of methane gas. The "window" around the upper deck must have been similar to a riding arena; since this deck was open, the ventilation would have been fairly good. The animals on board the ark must have been young but fully matured, because the earth's animal population was quickly restored after the flood.

It should be understood that the flood was not a storm. Storm conditions are not described anywhere in the text. God sent movements of air only after the continents had drained somewhat, to help the drying process. Imagine water on the North American continent rising to fifteen cubits, or twenty to twenty-five feet, above the highest hill at the time. Do you ever wonder how the Grand Canyon and similar valleys around the world were formed? It is likely that flood runoff was responsible for these formations.

Up to this point, I have briefly recounted the creation week. It is important to remember that every time the Bible mentions a day, it means a literal twenty-four-hour period. Any reference to a Bible "day" as signifying a longer period of time is inconsistent with context and reason. The creation account names a day as an evening and a morning, and only that specific time makes any sense. Just as it is foolish to claim that the human eye evolved.

Some Extra Observations on the Worldwide Flood as Described in Genesis

God, the ET creator, describes that the world before the flood was extremely wicked, and the thoughts of men were continually thinking up ways to do evil.

It seems that Noah was the only man, along with his family, that deserved not to be wiped off the earth. This does not necessarily mean that Noah and his kin were without sin; it simply means that Noah had a heart for good and walked with God.

Noah was directed to build an ark, a floating zoo, about two-thirds the size of the *Titanic*, three stories (decks) high, with a window encircling the top deck. There was obviously an overhang, or the lower decks would have been quickly flooded. This ark was to hold all kinds of animals.

Consider "kinds" for a minute. Modern breeding has produced many varieties of dogs, cats, horses, etc. There are a few breeds of dogs from which varieties come; dogs like wolf, dingo, African wild dog, fox, coyote, and hyena are a few of the possible kinds that came on board. Cats, lion, tiger, lynx, puma, leopard, cheetah, and possibly one or two kinds of domestic cat came on board.

With horses, there are three major kinds pictured on a vase from ancient China, from the dynasty of Emperor Wu-ti (156

BC). This vase shows a spotted variety (modern Appaloosa?), Arab (with high head carriage), and one other with barb characteristics.

Since I bred Appaloosas for fifteen years, I can confidently say that interbreeding between Appaloosa and Arab produces offspring with genetic deformities. The Arab kind has three fewer lumbar vertebrae than barb or Appaloosa and produces a deformity called wobblers, because the genetic code does not know which amount of vertebra to produce, resulting in the nerves of the spine not being intact and unable to send proper signals from the brain in order to control the hind quarters.

The result is something called wobblers. The offspring often dies young, and if the offspring lives past maturity, the problem shows up in subsequent generations.

Kinds as such can therefore be somewhat numerous.

Noah needed three floors (decks), each deck with rooms (stalls). One stall for a horse averages ten feet by ten feet; for dinosaurs, somewhat larger.

I consider wooly mammoth and mastodon to be two kinds.

So now the earth is dried after the flood. Men and animals emerge from the ark to devastation—or not.
All the people are gone. All the old plants are gone, and new plant life is already growing. The animals have plants to eat, and the carnivores have some of the offspring from those animals that came on board the ark in their sevens. But what happened to the plant life that was abundant on the earth before the rains began?

I recently saw in a news report that a new oil field in Utah has the potential to produce trillions of barrels of oil. This is where all the old plant life went. It was buried and became coal. Under pressure, coal will turn to oil in a short period of time, mere days, if not hours. This fact flies directly in the face of Darwin's evolutionary theory. This book deals in truth and fact, not theory. What if I were to say that creation took place within days and hours and I have faith that this is what happened? Is that faith so unreasonable compared with the faith of someone who believes that the universe just happened, by some unknown, unseen, incomprehensible force compressing all known substances into a compact mass, then exploding and "creating" the known universe?

All this was supposed to have happened in a vacuum. Soon after the Hubble telescope was launched, it was found that the galaxies on the outer edge of the universe were expanding at an increased rate away from a central point. This can't happen in a vacuum, unless there was more than one big bang. Then we have another problem. In high school chemistry, we learn that pressure produces heat; the more pressure, the more heat. The simple question is, then, how much heat would all the compressed substance of the universe produce when compacted into a beach ball–sized mass?

I'm sorry, but the laws of thermodynamics and hydrodynamics cannot be negated to make faith in evolution viable.

So Noah and his relatives emerged from the ark, probably a bit smelly at this point. Every life form known today, and those yet undiscovered, emerged to a remade earth. All the animals, birds, and creepy-crawlies started new. Of course, God did not have to put ocean creatures on the ark; these had life in the sea. Many sea creatures did die as a result of the worldwide upheaval, but most survived. Details of how the land animals distributed themselves on the new land are not given; all we know is that they safely disembarked the ark and were thriving.

Worldwide, many pits and masses of bones have been discovered, all jumbled together. Some of these piles contain as many as two dozen different kinds of bones. Museums around the world dig up and collect these bones, but in all these museums, there cannot be found one example of a transitional skeleton. *Archaeopteryx* is a bird and has been proven to be so. Coelacanth is a live-bearing fish, and Lucy is an incomplete skeleton of a ground ape with rickets. Piltdown Man was a fraud, made up by university pranksters. The Scopes trial, if held today, would be summarily thrown out of court, because *Australopithecus afarensis* is not a transitional skeleton, but another example of an ape.

Once again, we see God, Jehovah Elohim, taking part in creation by declaring to Noah and his family that the earth will never again suffer a worldwide flood. Noah had been spared because he walked with God and was genetically free from corruption by fallen angels and their giant offspring. This does not mean that sin was not present in his makeup. It was not long before his grandsons and granddaughters fell back into some of the preflood error.

God does not change. He only changes his methodology in dealing with us. After the flood, man is permitted to kill and eat animal flesh. Noah makes an altar and kills an offering; as the temple priests later in the Bible would kill and eat animal offerings, so does Noah in Genesis 8:20–21. This sacrifice is symbolic of the coming offering of Christ on the cross for our sins. We symbolically digest Christ's body at the sacrament.

In Genesis 9:8, we see God speaking to Noah to establish his covenant. In this instance, it would seem that God's voice is audible. A rainbow had never before been seen on earth, because no rain fell before the flood.

Good old Noah, the first thing he did to resume his life on the earth, or at least the first thing we are told about, was to plant a vineyard and get drunk. Noah must have already been familiar with farming, because this is the occupation he chose to take up after the flood. This could not have been a trial-and-error process, or his family would have become very hungry. Genesis 10 provides the genealogy of Noah and his sons; within four generations, they had spread through the entire Fertile Crescent, Turkey, and North Africa. A fantastic amount of information is omitted in the description of man's dispersion throughout these lands. It would have been unreasonable to follow all these individuals in their exploits. Only the individuals who made a name for themselves, whether famous or infamous, are depicted in detail.

CHAPTER 3

THE NEXT NOTABLE person described in the Old Testament is Noah's great-great-grandson Nimrod. He is important for a number of reasons, but for our purposes, mainly because he causes one of the most important extraterrestrial interventions before the Nativity star.

Nimrod, from the line of Cush, is said to be "a mighty hunter before the LORD" (Genesis 10:9). His lands were Babel, the site of early Babylon; all of Syria; and Akadia. The territory he ruled is laid out in Genesis 10:8–20. The term "mighty hunter before the LORD" denotes supreme arrogance, something like that of Saddam Hussein, but perhaps even greater. Four of the cities he had built were Babel, Erech, Accad, and Calneh. At least three, and possibly all four, of these cities have been unearthed by archaeologists. Recently, an unknown city dating to the time of Nimrod has been excavated. Within Nimrod's borders were the infamous cities of the plain, including Sodom and Gomorrah. These last two cities, along with others nearby, were definitely destroyed by extraterrestrial activity and angelic intervention.

While building the tower of Babel, and under the influence of his mother-wife, Nimrod decided to build a tower whose top was in the heavens or, as in the Received Text, "whose top may reach unto heaven" (11:4).

Stop here and consider; four generations after the sky fell and flooded the earth, we have a man whose arrogance led him to lead a workforce to build a tower. Why? As an altar? No, a man who would marry his own mother is not of the mind-set to honor God. Noah was still alive at this point and undoubtedly told his flood story over and over. Nimrod wasn't stupid; stupid people don't become leaders of men. Modern-day dictator Saddam only began to repair one city (Babylon), but Nimrod built many new cities. His arrogance and pride far surpassed Saddam's, and he knew that there was no reason to try to reach any literal heaven. And what would he do when the top of the tower literally broke through the clouds? No, this was not the tower's purpose according to the construction method.

I personally took a break from my harness shop for about three years and joined a gang of restoration workers whose projects included building stone fireplaces and refurbishing stonework and brickwork on period houses. We worked on the Bluestone House and cottage and many other old homes in Port Perry, Ontario, and around the country. One of our projects was restoring a log house. The timbers were square and had angled dovetails, a type of edging known as chamfering. It is superstrong and must have been the method Noah used to build the ark's corners. The point is, I have a good idea how construction works, as well as when and why different methods are used.

I believe that Nimrod and his gang got together and decided to make a radio beacon that would reach deep space. Nimrod assumed, as do ancient astronaut theorists such as Erich von Däniken, that God or "the gods" were reachable by a radio or a transmitter. In Genesis 11, they start to build, and I'm sure that a careful analysis of their building instructions will shed light on their purpose. Chapter 11:3 tells us that the builders declared, "Let us make brick, and burn them thoroughly." This says volumes. First, if they were making a tower of brick, then they were not planning on building it superhigh, because brick alone will not support even an edifice as tall as Khufu's Pyramid. Second, if the bricks were baked, they would burn and come out of the oven with a glassy surface. So the builders had bricks with a glassy surface mortared with slime. This would produce a very thin joint, almost nonexistent. The tower started to come together. What they were building was a gigantic radio tower for sending and receiving messages from heaven, or the heavens. That Nimrod and his gang of thugs ended up producing was a tower with similar to the cryptal radio sets we made as kids in the 40's and 50's. Ultimately, Nimrod and his gang were fascinated with the power that could be obtained from the fallen sons of God, whom we have already discussed.

At this point, another extraterrestrial intervention occurred and foiled their plans. I often wonder if the builders were actually successful in contacting God, and he answered by sending an electric signal to the tower and scrambling human speech with an electric shock wave. Whatever happened, the tower seemed to have worked; human speech was scrambled, and the workers and other citizens of Nimrod's kingdom dispersed.

Nimrod, Semiramis, and their gang certainly had their theological-egotistical problems. Nimrod was a postflood gangster as indicated by the name "mighty hunter before the LORD." Semiramis was a truly ambitious woman, marrying her own son. Obviously, Noah's good graces and closeness with the Creator did not rub off on these two.

From the description of the building methods employed in making the tower, or radio beacon, it was clearly meant to contact someone or something in space. What caused the extraterrestrial contact in Genesis 11:5, "The LORD came down"? Was this a coincidence, just Jehovah doing his monthly rounds of the earth? "Trinity, it's time we checked in on man, let's go and see how they are coming along"? I don't think so.

I believe that Nimrod's radio beacon-tower actually contacted the heavens and alerted Jehovah that something was amiss and needed to be investigated. What does God do? He summons the Trinity, and they pay Nimrod and company a visit. What happens next is a cataclysm akin to the Manhattan Project. God scrambles their radio signals, and their brains start getting their own signals crossed. The people then disperse because they no longer speak the same language. At this point, I'm sure that all the races went their own ways and fled to the earth's four corners.

CHAPTER 4

BEFORE WE MOVE on from Nimrod and his mother-wife, let us make a brief excursion into Egypt. On the Giza Plateau are many pyramids, some small and others not so small. Many theories abound as to who built them, when, and why. Mr. Hawass, of Egyptian antiquities fame, would have us believe that they were actually built by the men for whom they have been named. I'm not so sure; the mathematics just doesn't add up. Khufu's Pyramid would have to have been laid at the rate of one stone every couple of minutes or less to have been completed in the time specified.

The Egyptian pyramids were not tombs. No complete mummy has ever been found in one. Grave robbers left bones scattered, but not in the pyramids. If they are tombs, what are all the mummies doing in the Valley of the Kings and the Valley of the Queens? Why have no funerary cones been found in any pyramids, only in the Theban Necropolis? I need much more convincing.

There is a book on the market titled *A Compendium of Egyptian Funerary Cones,* written by Gary Dibley, Bron Lipkin, and Julie Masquelier-Loorius. In my e-mail correspondence with Mr. Dibley, he would not commit to the pyramids being tombs. All known cones came from the valleys. On close examination, we see that the Pharaohs had the same ego problem as Nimrod and were obsessed with contacting God or the gods. The very name for the structures they built, pyramids, tells us that some sort of fire, either physical, electrical, or solar, was produced inside them. My own conclusion is that this was electrical fire.

There is absolutely no ash residue inside the pyramids from torches or burning material, neither is there any residue from solar activity.

Above the Queen's Chamber in the Great Pyramid are two massive blocks of red granite positioned in the same way as the quartz crystals in your wristwatch. Other conduits have copper embedded in the granite. Sometime soon, if Mr. Hawass allows, we may find that Egyptians produced electrical currents on a massive scale, either in an attempt to talk to "God" or to produce levitation with magnetism and sound.

Nimrod's tower was a bust because of extraterrestrial intervention. But this did not stop Semiramis in her ambitions. She was the real force behind Nimrod. Because God denied her direct access to his throne, she did the next best thing in her own eyes. She declared that she was queen of heaven, no less. When Nimrod died, she declared that his body was transported to the North Star. When Semiramis herself died, she had the priestesses declare that her body had been transported to the Pleiades. The "queen of heaven" tradition, a product of one woman's arrogance, is carried on today in some religions; such arrogance.

The nation of Egypt was already established by the time the next part of our story took place. Much time had passed, and the human experimentation continued.

Genesis 11:10–12:3 contain another genealogy, as well as God's order to Abram to "get thee out of thy country" (Genesis 12:1). I'm sure that many other people who worked on the tower of Babel were smart enough to do the same. The story that follows depicts the birth of the Jewish nation and of their troubles in the Middle East. An extraterrestrial event took place when the Lord physically appeared to Abram with the promise that he would sire a great nation.

Little has been said in the last few pages of any extraterrestrial activity. But let's consider Necho for a bit. He is interesting, because he is ambitious, building a trireme fleet to go round Africa to bolster and reestablish trade routes. He starts but does not complete a canal at Suez. Necho was a latecomer when it comes to building a canal at Suez. The project was attempted half a dozen times previously, the first attempt being around 2000 BC. This is about the time Abraham founded Judaism and the Stonehenge was supposed to have been built. The Hebrews were gone from Egypt long ago. So we don't know for sure who was conscripted to do the work. For sure, it was not transformers or clones, as depicted in the Noah's ark movie! Any such attempt tells me Necho was a "mover," not a looser. Necho led many campaigns against the Babylonians and captured the fabled Kadesh. The Babylonians prevailed, and the Hebrews all went into captivity under Nebuchadnezzar— another prophesied extraterrestrial event. I mean, who can know this so far in advance? Who can give Ezekiel the knowledge to make this "assumption"? Only an extraordinary god who lives from infinity to infinity.

He described himself to Moses, from the bush that was not consumed. Moses asks, "Whom shall I say sent me?" and God answers, "Eh'je a'ser eh'je sent you." This is an accurate translation: I will prove to be whom I will prove to be or I am from everlasting to everlasting, your ever-present extraterrestrial—one of a kind. Not Buddha, Baal, Allah, or Confucius. Not Ashtaroth. Not Lao-tzu. Not some unnamed god or prophet or teacher. But the Creator God who broke into history as a man through God's personal intervention and called him Jesus. "This is my beloved son in whom I am well pleased."

All the rest of us are just pawns who have the right to follow this extraterrestrial we know as Jehovah, or not, but let's continue with more history and try to find more extraterrestrial activity.

Abram's side trek to Egypt brought him into contact with a powerful Pharaoh. The Old Kingdom was in full swing, and the Pharaoh at the time was most likely Djoser (Zoser). This man had a second in command called Imhotep. A seven-year famine is recorded during Djoser's reign, so Imhotep is most likely Joseph. The Old Kingdom period in Egypt saw the building of many step pyramids, overseen by Joseph, but we will return to his story as we continue through the biblical text. For now, let's examine the stories of Abram and his nephew Lot. The story of Lot is crammed full of extraterrestrials, so we'll consider it in some detail.

CHAPTER 5

GOD GAVE CANAAN to Abram. After all, it was Jehovah God who created all the earth, so he can give it, or portions of it, to whomever he pleases. The plan was to provide a savior for mankind through Abram's race.

In the meantime, Lot and Abram came to an agreement as to the division of the land of Canaan. Lot chose the well-watered land around Sodom and Gomorrah, while Abram went north. Lot made a bad choice. In Genesis 14, warring kings (tribal warlords) from Shinar, Ellasar, and Elam come against Sodom and Gomorrah and the cities of the plain. Lot becomes a prisoner of war. Upon hearing of this, Abram raises an army, attacks the warlords, and rescues Lot. After Lot's rescue, Jehovah Elohim promises Abram, whom he renames Abraham, that all the land from the Nile to the Euphrates is for his inheritance. This is basically the entire Fertile Crescent. Note that this land was given to Abraham, not to Hamas or Boko Haram or ISIS.

Lot's story is now put briefly on hold as the Old Testament takes up the story of the birth of the Arab nation. Up to this point, God has been speaking to Abraham in dreams, visions, and audibly. Abraham is an old man now, and we read of extraterrestrial activity in Genesis 18. The Lord appeared to Abraham as he was sitting in his tent door. Two "men" were with him. So here we have the Lord and two companions visiting Abraham. Abraham offers them hospitality and refreshment. Abraham and Sarah make a banquet (wouldn't you if angels visited?), and the messengers give Abraham a promise that a great nation will be born to them. Mind reading is a concept we associate with extraterrestrial activity; Sarah had a good laugh about the promise privately, but the Lord knew her thoughts.

In the meantime, while the Lord and two friends are sojourning with Abraham and Sarah, our good friend Lot is getting into trouble again. It seems that he can't avoid the "lure of the bright lights," and he moves closer and closer to the depraved city of Sodom. When the biblical narrative picks up Lot's story, he has his dwelling inside the Sodom city gates.

It seems that there was a dual purpose for the Lord's visit to Abraham. The men, or rather the angels, start heading toward Sodom. Meanwhile, the Lord tells Abraham of Sodom's impending doom. Apparently, the city's sin is great and has drawn in most of the inhabitants. The nature of this sin is not immediately apparent, but the conversation between the Lord and Abraham indicates that Sodom will soon be destroyed because of it. The conversation concludes with the Lord's pledge that if there is only one righteous family in Sodom, then the city will not be destroyed.

When the angels get to Sodom, Lot is not in the city, but at the gate. Lot recognizes the angels for what they are and greets them accordingly. This is somewhat strange, because we are not given any information to the effect that Lot had previous encounters with extraterrestrials. In any case, Lot is encouraged to gather his family and flee the coming destruction. Lot entreats the angels to stay as house guests. They do so. Within minutes, the men of Sodom rush Lot's house and demand that he send the "men" out so that they might "know them." The word *know* here is genteel Bible speak for "sodomize." Here, then, we come face-to-face with the grave sin for which Sodom was to be destroyed, but not Sodom alone. Also to be wiped out were Gomorrah, Admah, Bela, and Zeboim, these being the other cities of the plain. We are told that the area around these cities abounded with tar pits, and tar burns very well.

Lot intercedes for the angels, as though they really needed any help, by offering his daughters to the crowd instead of the "men." As I see it, this was the ultimate insult to the Sodomites; men with a depraved preference for their own sex over female companionship must have been incensed by Lot's suggestion. They tried to break down the door. During the scuffle, the extraterrestrial angels caused every man and boy near the door to become blind—perhaps with some kind of pepper spray?

In any case, the angels hustle Lot and his family out of the city while the men are blinded. Lot's family had to put on heavy garments, perhaps to protect themselves against the destruction. We can only surmise, but during the atomic blast at Hiroshima, people had their light clothing burned completely off. If the blast that finished Sodom was an atomic-type blast, and there is every indication that it was, then heavy garments would give some protection. Lot's wife turned to see the destruction and was turned to a "pillar of salt"; this also indicates an atomic blast.

Remember, the writers described events as they saw them in 2000 BC, so we must be a little forgiving of their description. Whatever the exact cause of the destruction, the tar pits must also have burned furiously. There are no archaeological records of these cities, only textual records.

One note here: sodomy is described in the Received Texts of the Bible as a sin against the Creator, as is its companion sin, lesbianism. Engaging in either of these sins is a conscious choice. Jehovah God made the Creation one day at a time and pronounced every day's work good. After he created man and woman, he pronounced this work "very good." Nowhere, but nowhere, is there any indication that he made a gay gene just to mess with things. Modern medicine has been searching for such a gene, but it isn't there in the Bible. Sorry, guys, but you're going to have to synthesize one and lie about it.

CHAPTER 6

THE NEXT FEW chapters of Genesis contain many instances of extraterrestrials. Every place an "angel" or "angel of the Lord" is mentioned, we see God, in one form or another, interacting with his creation. The entire Old Testament is filled with this sort of thing. I hope that you will read the Received Texts in a new light and search out these truths.

It is imperative to use texts originating in Antioch, not Alexandria. Alexandrian texts are based on the Sinaiticus, Vaticanus, and the LXX, better known as the Septuagint. The Septuagint is supposed to have been written around the time of Ptolemy Soter, also known as Philadelphus, but no one is certain. There is a rumor circulating out of the Vatican that this pre-Christian document is extant—it is not. The only two known copies are in the British Museum and the Vatican. Both copies were written by a Roman Catholic monk by the name of Origen. This man was writing under duress. The copy in the Vatican has at least fourteen hands correcting it. Origen is touted as a "church father," but he did not believe that Jesus rose bodily from the grave. He believed in reincarnation, but he did not believe that Jesus was virgin-born. He did not believe that the Holy Spirit is a person. This man was the original Jehovah's Witness. His teacher was Eusebius, and most of his work influenced Jerome and was undertaken for Constantine the Great.

Constantine himself was not a Christian, let alone the first Christian emperor. If he was ever "saved," his life never showed it. There is no evidence of Christian symbols on his arch, coins, or buildings. He certainly had lots of time to prove his Christianity. He was a young man when he saw the "sign in the sky" before the Milvian Bridge at his defeat of Maxentius. Since his life remained unchanged by this portent, what "sign" did he actually see? Historical carvings of the time show a modified ankh, a pagan fertility symbol.

But you say his mother wrote his biography and she must have had the details correct. Wrong. Helena was a Druid temple priestess, and Druids never wrote anything. If we are to rely on "tradition" for our history lessons, it must not contradict history. The Roman church claims that Constantine was baptized on his deathbed. Good news, guys, nobody, but nobody, gets saved by being baptized. Salvation comes only from a personal relationship with the Savior, Jesus Christ—baptism is only an acknowledgment of the life change.

One other note on Constantine: After winning the Battle of the Milvian Bridge, he set up a pope in Rome by the name of Damasus. Soon afterward, he moved his capital to Constantinople and set himself up as the first pope of the Eastern Roman Empire. Not long after that, he set up a third pope in Alexandria.

I count three popes at the same time. This is history, not tradition. Which are you going to believe? Here, then, are the beginnings of the true Roman Catholic Church. Peter was never the first pope. Peter's own words deny this emphatically. In 1 Peter 2, he admonishes Christians to come to Christ, the living stone. Believe in Christ, not Peter. Christ is precious. He is the living stone that men rejected but whom God chose. Peter is not that stone, and he affirms this. Christ becomes the chief cornerstone, the first and basic building block of his own church—not Peter, or any pope for that matter.

So Constantine built a church on himself and on other popes, and this all happened in the late third century AD. By reading true history, we see that James, brother of Jesus, was the first bishop (not pope) of the real Christian church. Many Christian church leaders were killed in the first three centuries by Constantine's forefathers and other men like them. Real history is still available for all laymen and Christian pastors who care to dig for it, and not merely accept tradition as spoon-fed to the masses by reigning popes and Vatican councils. Vatican II has never closed the office of the Inquisition, and the current pope is its current head.

But that is enough diversion. My main objective is to list the extraterrestrial happenings in the Bible, so let's get back to it.

Returning to Genesis, we proceed past a few well-known Sunday school stories about Abraham and his son Isaac and how God spoke audibly to prevent the boy's death and about Sarah's death and burial in Canaan. Isaac grows to maturity and the "angel of the Lord" aids in finding a bride for him. Genesis 25 records the death of Abraham, the genealogy of Ishmael, and some episodes from the life of Isaac's sons, Jacob and Esau. The next extraterrestrial event recorded in Genesis seems insignificant, but is actually quite important.

It seems that there was another famine, but this time Isaac was told by God not to go to Egypt. The Old Kingdom was coming to an end, but God wanted Isaac to put down roots in Canaan. The stories that follow are further familiar Sunday school material, until Genesis 30:37. Isaac's son Jacob uses tree branches to somehow genetically alter the sheep and goats of Laban's flock so that they change color. The resulting speckled and spotted animals are to be added to his own herd. How was this done?

We aren't sure; however, if anything is true of genetics, it is that there are many variables, and I speculate that Jacob was a keen observer. While breeding horses, my chosen breed was the Appaloosa. Spots and speckles are one genetic variant, and it's very possible to mate two solid-colored horses and have the offspring emerge with spots, blotches, or the most-preferred blanket pattern. This coat pattern consists of white hind quarters with spots.

ROBIN WARD

Many circuses have horse acts with spotted horses. One instance is a horse called wapiti. This was a registered quarter horse until he was five years old. One spring, when he shed his winter coat, there it was—a huge white blanket on his hind end with numerous dark brown spots. His quarter horse registration papers were pulled immediately, and he was re-registered as an Appaloosa. (I have pictures to prove it.) This is not to say that creation is still happening, only that variations within a kind can take place. Breeding outside a kind always ends in a dead end.

Just what the tree branches did in this case, we aren't told, except to say that extraterrestrial intervention is mentioned. Minor extraterrestrial events occur till we meet Joseph (Imhotep) in Genesis 37. Joseph was a dreamer, and early on in his life, we hear of a dream that comes true later on, about his future greatness. It seems that Joseph became a great builder under Zoser. As Imhotep, he was the overseer in the building of the step pyramid and many other step pyramids in the Old Kingdom.

Joseph's story is one of the best-known Sunday school stories in the Bible. There is no point rehashing the whole thing. Donny Osmond certainly did a good job with his stage production *Joseph and the Amazing Technicolor Dreamcoat.*

How did Joseph get to be a dreamer whose dreams came true? For this, we have to go back to the extraterrestrial intervention of God. See Genesis 35:10. God, the extraterrestrial, tells Jacob (Israel) that kings will come out of his body. In other words, his offspring will have extraordinary powers. This certainly was the case with Joseph. History and tradition both agree on this point. History records a seven-year famine in Egypt during the reign of Djoser (Zoser). Joseph's family joins him in Egypt, and Pharaoh gives them the best land in the Nile Delta to raise their flocks. So ends Genesis. And Joseph dies, being 110 years old. He was embalmed (mummified?) and put in a coffin. We are not told where he was buried, but most certainly not in a pyramid, because he was next to royalty. It's likely his place is somewhere in the Valley of the Kings.

In my possession is a funerary cone, one of only 611 known to exist. The purpose of which is unknown. From my study of these, I have come to the conclusion that they were the 2500 BC equivalent of sympathy cards.

From the description on them, I find the Bible records written by Moses and the sentiment expressed at the death of certain men and women in the texts. These sentiments and those on Egyptian funerary cones are strikingly similar.

Many circuses have horse acts with spotted horses. Once such act featured an animal named Wapiti. He was a registered quarter horse until he was five years old. One spring, he shed his winter coat and there it was – a huge "white blanket" on his hind end with numerous dark brown spots. His quarter horse registration papers were pulled immediately, and he was re-registered as an Apaloosa.

CHAPTER 7

NOW THE JEWS are in Egypt, under a new Pharaoh that was not familiar with Joseph's contributions to the country. This new Pharaoh must have been a conqueror from a different country. Not able to read the Egyptian records, or not caring, it doesn't matter much for our purpose.

Fact is, the Hebrews were made into slaves and came under great duress. Orders were given that midwives were to kill or see to it that male children of the Hebrews were killed.

The power of this type of dictator needed special attention. The texts only tell us that God, in some extraordinary way, "deals with the midwives." It seems the midwives feared (and obeyed) God more than Pharaoh, so many male children survived.

Moses was one of them. His adoptive mother was Pharaoh's daughter, and we all know the story. How he was taken in to Pharaoh's house and was tutored there. I would expect he got the equivalent of today's master's degree or similar.

Moses has a number of extraterrestrial encounters. First is the burning bush. Somehow the bush was not consumed, and the voice of Jehovah emanated from it.

I remember an experiment done at John Hopkins, in the '50s, where students tried to simulate messages transferred through a burning flame. They succeeded, and an audible voice message was transmitted from another part of the university.

Moses was compelled to remove his shoes. This could have been necessary as part of the "transmission" of the voice. Was it Jehovah speaking? Yes, for sure. We have seen how messages can be transmitted by using crystals. As a kid in the '50s, I knew how a crystal radio set worked. Certainly God is able to use our physical world to his advantage.

With Moses standing barefoot on granite (crystals) or sand (more crystalline), the voice was sure to be clearer.

The temple priests stood in the sand with the ephod around their necks when they "talked to God," and they also had gold thread woven into their garments—living receivers of God's voice? More on that later.

Moses listened and watched as the "finger of God" cut two tablets of stone and "wrote the Ten Commandments" on them.

Why should we be surprised not to suppose God can produce laser light anywhere and at any time he wants in order to get the message out? God made light way back in Genesis 1. Who are we to suspect laser light was not one of the types of light included in that creative act? Can we suppose that evolution could do it?

So Moses smashes the first set. God makes another set. Now granite is not light, and I'm sure Moses had no easy task carrying the granite slabs down the mountain. Moses is told by God that he, God, will use Moses as his tool to get the people back into the Promised Land.

Don't forget that God promised Canaan and the Fertile Crescent to the Hebrews, not to the offspring of Ishmael. Ishmael's offspring were also to be a great nation, but not in the Promised Land.

Moses got the message. He didn't like it, and he objected. God persisted. Moses went to see Pharaoh.

Time has passed. Moses is now a grown man. Pharaohs have come and gone. We (and Hollywood) suppose that Moses pleads his case to Ramses the Great. To prove this to Pharaoh, God tells Moses to throw his staff on the ground. It becomes a serpent. When he takes it by the tail, it becomes a rod again. Moses gets an audience with Pharaoh and throws Aaron's staff down, and it becomes a snake.

This next part always intrigued me—Pharaoh calls his magicians, Jannes and Jambres, over. They also do the same thing. Was this the norm in Egypt? No wonder Egypt was a powerful nation. Since they had guys that could transmute matter, they also brought up frogs.

Does this give us some idea that possibly some other tricks, like levitation, were available to them? Is this a technology that we, moderns, need to relearn? Could men like the builder of the Coral Castle help us relearn this? Levitation seems the only possible way the large pyramids could have been completed in the time specified—do the math.

God's serpent ate the other two and became a rod again. But here we obviously have some extraterrestrial technology at work. Call it miracles if you like, but I still give credit to God, who can produce these happenings.

Ten plagues follow. All the first nine, I have seen explained scientifically—but not the tenth. Every firstborn, of men and cattle and pets, is touched by the death angel. The Passover is instituted, and the people are released. Approximately three million start their trek away from Goshen in the Nile Delta.

They follow a pillar of light at night and a cloud of smoke during the day. I have not heard a scientific explanation here. When they reach the Gulf of Aqaba, they seem caught, and here again, I have not heard a reasonable explanation for the waters of the Gulf being parted. Yes, I know about the wind and the shallow shelf they crossed over, which was *dry*—but I spent almost four years in the late '60s sailing in the Caribbean and Bahamas. I have seen sixty-plus-foot waves in the Gulf Stream. One calmer day, our crew observed an *Architeuthis* no more than twenty feet from our boat. It was at least forty feet long, with eyes as big as dinner plates.

All this time, I never once saw water stand straight up. The Pharaoh's army followed best they could, but the wheels fell off the chariots. I have an ex-harness maker's explanation why they fell off, having worked with leather for the better part of twenty-five years, but space prohibits. Needless to say, the wheels did fall off. There are chariot wheels (lots) on the Gulf floor, just where the Bible says they should be. What's more, there is a pillar that Moses erected on the East Bank commemorating the occasion.

Does God have a sense of humor? You bet. See Genesis 14:25. The Egyptians' chariot wheels fell off, and they drove them with *difficulty*. You bet they did; not at all, I think God, the extraterrestrial, keeps going, just like the add—going and going.

Moses is not done. The children of Israel keep complaining and crabbing about their situation in the desert. God tells them the original refugees will die there. Only the children born during the forty-year trek will get to enter Canaan. We see the people fed by extraterrestrial intervention—manna, quails, the battle with the Amalekites, water in abundance for drinking. Their survival was assured.

Moses, with council from Jethro, his father-in-law, organized a type of governing body, or bodies, to oversee the people's needs on a more personal basis. Since Jethro is assumed to be black and Moses married Jethro's daughter, we have the first mixed marriage. I only mention this here because he had two sons. These two sons would, arguably, have had offspring similar to Jamaicans or present-day Middle Eastern races.

Moses takes the people to Mount Sinai where they witness thunderings, lightning and smoke, and a thick darkness. Moses is the only one to approach God. God tells Moses in no uncertain terms that idols are *not* acceptable under any circumstances. After giving Moses specific laws concerning servants, property, etc., he gives an angel (possibly Jesus in preincarnate form?) to keep these people on the "straight and narrow."

On entering the land, the Israelites find there are ungodly nations established. These nations are to be cut off, and more specifically, the Hebrews are not to worship the other people's gods. God, the extraterrestrial, tells them that he will drive these other nations out of the Fertile Crescent with *hornets*. Why the hornets did not bother the Hebrews is only for God to know. Now we get an interesting account. Moses, Nadab, Abihu, and seventy elders of Israel go up Sinai and see God, the extraterrestrial. He appears to these men in Exodus 24:9–12. His face must have been hidden, because there is no description, but they saw his feet standing on what appeared to be a sapphire roadway. Some commentators say this is symbolic of God having the nations of the world under his feet.

Nevertheless, it's just one more extraterrestrial event recorded in the Old Testament—and who's to say we shouldn't think on these things? After all, God wrote the *whole* Bible for our benefit. Chapter 26 now tells us specifically how the priests' garments are to be made. Going on through chapter 28, we end up with priestly vestments that give us the trappings of guys decked out to be literally radio receivers—gold wires (antennae), ephod containing one crystal for each tribe, Urim and Thummim (two other larger crystals that can be used for fine-tuning incoming messages), a gold bell (loud speaker?), gold rings that could be "radio" dials—is it starting to make sense?

So far we have almost everything but the spacecraft, if one is needed. God, being omnipresent, doesn't need one. However, how do his messengers get from place to place? Read on.

Gold thread woven into the ephod is described in chapter 39. The complete description of the building of the Tabernacle is described. The Hebrews only proceeded in their travels under God's direct command, thus ends Exodus.

CHAPTER 8

L EVITICUS GETS ITS name from the tribe if Levi, who provided the priestly leaders for the Hebrews. The Levites were very strict in their dealings with the people, and they gave many written instructions about health and worship of God. Two of Aaron's sons decided to take matters into their own hands and worship God in their own way. Chapter 10:2 says fire went out from the Lord and devoured them.

What's happening here? In verse 6, Moses tells those present not to uncover their heads or cause any part of their body to be exposed at this time. Isn't this the same thing the two angels told Lot and his family to be wary of while fleeing Sodom? Could this "fire" from God, from the cloud that was present above the Tabernacle, been phaser fire or electrostatic discharge? Whatever it was, the two guys were dead. Specific instructions were to carry them out, by their tunics, not to touch the bodies directly, lest there be some contamination that was transferable.

Lots of advice (laws) were given for health, sanitation, clean and unclean foods. They are outlined in detail over the next few chapters. It seems that leprosy was rampant around the area. There are moral laws about not cheating and being fair with your neighbors. We are told not to cut the flesh or tattoo the body, not to regard mediums or familiar spirits, to avoid male-male and female-female relations because they are an *abomination* to the Lord.

Chapter 21 gives specific outlines for worship by priests. This is specifically why no Levite would allow heads of tribes to travel to Egypt to translate the so-called Septuagint for the Ptolemys.

The Egyptians and especially the Egyptian priests did not keep any of the laws laid out in the previous twenty chapters. Egyptian priests not only tattooed their bodies but also painted them all colors, just see the tombs. Their gods were *not* the god of the Bible, and their rituals were profane, to the sacrificing of infants and malformed. The gods they worshiped were dead wood and stone, unable to speak, think, or reason—without souls (psyche).

As far as the Septuagint is concerned, any pre-Christian 300 BCE Septuagint does not exist—never did. I have read all the works of Josephus, at least twice, and if he mentioned such a writing as existing in 300 BC, I can't find it. All we have is tradition that says it existed, because the Roman Catholic church father Origen is supposed to have seen it, memorized it word for word, and made two copies of it.

Any historian or priest or theologian I have contacted that tells me it is extant cannot tell me where the extant copy is housed. The two copies by Origen, I count as fakes and, from his hand, are dated to his time and that of Eusebius in the late third CCE.

I propose that all so-called bibles that use this spurious document and other Alexandrian writings, such as the Sinaiticus and Vaticanus, be scrapped by real Christian churches worldwide.

CHAPTER 9

TWO SPIES CONVINCE the congregation that this truly is a land of milk and honey. A futile invasion is launched under their own initiative. The Ark of the Covenant, Moses, and Aaron are not included in this action, and it fails— so what happens? They start complaining again, and some offer incense to idols. God's fire consumes them. These guys just don't get it; they complain even more.

God tells Moses to get a rod (staff) from each tribe and put them in the Tabernacle. God will choose the leaders of the invasion by making one staff to blossom. Levi is chosen because Aaron is the head of the house of Levi.

More purification laws follow, and the congregation starts to move again toward Canaan. On the way, Moses gets angry and strikes the rock to get water, instead of touching it. This time it's Moses who gets the word that he can't enter the Promised Land. Shortly thereafter, the people again speak against God and Moses and are plagued with snakebites so that many died. Moses to the rescue. He makes the likeness of a snake, at God's instruction. Anyone looking at the snake on a pole is miraculously cured.

Different kings, I like to call them warlords, are defeated as the Israelites move north. The warlord Balak tries to get the jump on the Israelites by calling on a wizard named Balaam to curse the Israelites. Here, we see the attempted trial of one extraterrestrial force against another—God the Creator. It backfires when a donkey speaks against the wizard, telling him that the road was blocked. Balaam's eyes were "opened," and suddenly he saw the angel of the Lord (Jesus, in one of his preforms). Jesus was holding a flaming sword. Could this have been a literal sword? Yes. Possibly something akin to a lightsaber as in *Star Wars*?

Whatever it was, we can't be sure. One thing that is certain, dumb animals can see more than humans. The donkey saw Jesus, and Balaam didn't, so is this a once-in-a-lifetime vision, or do all animals see more than we give them credit for, all the time?

Balaam starts to open up vocally and denounces Balak and continues by giving a brief revue of coming events for Balak's kingdom. The congregation continues to make headway in Canaan and more instructions for keeping a theocratic state. The borders of the conquered land are given—it seems to include most of the western Fertile Crescent, including the West Bank into Egypt, to the Nile, including Gaza and part of western Iran.

The book of Numbers ends with rules for marriage of female heirs and instructions to marry within each one's tribe so there will be no dispute over money.

CHAPTER 10

IN LEVITICUS 26, we see God making promises of blessing to the Hebrews for their obedience. But he also is very aggravated at their continued wavering and ends up saying, "It's going to be my way, or the highway." Literally, they will be scattered among the nations of the world. They didn't, and he did. Thus ends Levi's messages.

Numbers

My NKJV says, in the intro to Numbers, that the pre-Christian Septuagint (nonexistent) was completed about 150 BCE. Here, we have a problem. As I previously mentioned, the document was supposed to be extant in the third century BCE and copied by Origen. However, tradition says that it was completed by Hebrew priests in their lifetime, about 300 BCE, for Ptolemy Philadelphus, and housed in the Alexandrian library. This is odd indeed. How can my NKJV and tradition both be correct, when there is at least one hundred years between the two dates? I say they are *both* wrong, according to my research. How much credibility can I ascribe to other notes in this edition?

But, onward and upward. Numbers is a book of numbers. As such, since God is its author, who are we to argue? Numbers 1:36 gives a number of 603,550, which suggests a population of around three million. This is the number (approximate) of people of the Exodus.

Since God saw to it, the original population of the Exodus did not see the Promised Land, and since the average family increases by doubling itself every ten years (a generation), it is *entirely* possible this number is accurate.

Chapter 5 gives a detailed account of dealing with unfaithful wives and punishment. Nowhere is there any punishment laid out for the men. Why?

We do not find any extraterrestrial activity in Numbers until chapter 9. The cloud above the Tabernacle appeared as fire-like in appearance and moved from place to place. Chapter 12 continues with God's children doing more and more complaining. God gets fed up and causes "fire" to come from the "cloud" they are following and burn some of them. Chapter 12 tells again that Moses had married an Ethiopian woman. Is this the first mixed marriage in history? If so, God does not speak against it. Instead he causes Miriam, one of the segregationists, to become leprous, requiring a time of cleansing and restitution. In this case, the leprosy was extraterrestrially condoned and produced. Miriam recants and is allowed back into the camp.

The saga is coming to a close. On the outskirts of the Promised Land, the congregation stops, and plans are made to spy the land. When the spies enter Canaan, they find many people of *large* stature. These people are descendants of Anak as well as the Amalekites, Hittites, Jebusites, and of course, Canaanites.

The Canaanites are notoriously evil beyond measure (see your best websites for details). Since God is a jealous and just god, who can blame him for ordering a genocide?

The sons of Anak—Anakim—are some descendants of the interbreeding of the "sons of God" and the daughters of men. This being the case, one or more of Noah's sons must not have been genetically free from interbreeding with "sons of God" (fallen angels).

But here they are, posing a threat to God's tribe and Moses. Ten of the spies oppose entering the land, but two of the twelve return with a cluster of grapes that could only be carried on a pole between two of them. Certainly this must give some indication of the abundance of plant life before the flood and give some credibility to the reason we find so much of this plant life preserved as *oil*.

CHAPTER 11

DEUTERONOMY, FROM *DUO,* or "second law"—this is the pre-Christian explanation of the name, meaning "second law," as taken from the pre-Christian Septuagint. I must reiterate: there is no such document and never was.

Think for a minute. Tradition says emphatically that the Roman Catholic father saw it and read it and memorized it and made two copies. The Septuagint is supposed to have been translated (a translation of the Hebrew writings) in or about 300 BCE for the Ptolemys. As tradition goes, Ptolemy is supposed to have gotten six scholars from each tribe (total of seventy-two) to come to Egypt to translate the Hebrew Scriptures into Greek.

The tribes, other than the Levites, did not have access to these writings. The Levites would *not* allow this undertaking. Even if they did pull it off, the Alexandrian libraries and compendia have been burned many times before Origen was born, notable burners being Julius Caesar and Nero, to name two. By the time Origen came on the scene, there was *no* pre-Christian Septuagint to memorize. He obviously invented his work to satisfy his sponsor and tutor, Constantine and Eusebius, respectively.

This being said (again), there is *no* "second law" in this book. Did Moses write it? Some say no but don't give any good alternative. Moses was certainly lettered well enough to write it, so don't strain at gnats.

The texts continue with Moses's directions in appointing tribal leaders. The conquest of Canaan again broaches the problem of giants. This time, the term *Emim* is used as a subgroup of Anakim. The term *Zamzumimm* is also used. It seems these guys are for real. These giants seem to be a remnant of the interbreeding of the rebel (fallen) angels and the daughters of men. This being the case, is it any wonder God lets the Israelites conquer them one by one? God intends to rid the earth of these genetic misfits and does so. The giants were infamous for idolatry and many other evils previously recounted. It seems that any manmade object that does not eat, hear, or smell can be considered an idol. Moses must be the author here. The Ten Commandments are reviewed, and chapter 6:4 specifically lays out what God was trying to say when he wrote them.

Particularly notice chapter 13. Instructions are specific to anyone wishing, or be enticed, to follow a prophet. Is that man a prophet of God? Details for determining such cannot be misinterpreted. Here, we pause to consider a point that is debated. In Deuteronomy 31:16, God the Creator tells Moses he will soon sleep with his fathers. This term is used over and over again from here to Malachi. The term is misquoted in the Alexandrian texts as "rest"—not the same as we will see later.

Chapter 32 recounts six times that Jesus is the rock of our salvation (not Peter). We know this is Jesus because "god" is referred to as a three-person unit. Romans 8:11 (and others) says the Holy Spirit raised Jesus from the dead. In John 2:19, Jesus says he will raise himself, not the Father, not the Holy Spirit, but "Me, me, me, and in my body to boot."

But we all know that God raised Jesus. How can the Trinity be denied when we consider Jesus can't lie?

This brief side trip into the extraterrestrial was needed, because Deuteronomy doesn't have much of this. Moses dies on Mount Nebo without entering the Promised Land. There is no accounting as to what happened to his body. It was never found. Since Moses appears on the Mount of Transfiguration with Jesus and Isaiah, we must assume that he is one of up to six humans transported to heaven. More on this later.

Errata

Let's take a minute or two for a breather and consider a TV show that first aired last night. I am writing the morning after, on July 8, 2014. The show was called *Big History*. It aired not on the History Channel but on the National Geographic Channel. The title is a misnomer and should be called the big lie or the big effort to confuse the naive.

That said, the show starts by showing Hitler (remember him?) at his chalet in the Alps. So far so good. Hitler did in fact have a chalet in the Alps. The next scene shows a German U-boat firing a torpedo; from there the lies begin. But the lies are mixed with some truth and a lot of computer-generated graphics. Immediately after the shot of the torpedo firing, the narrator says that Germany ruled the seas. No, Germany did *not*! This is the first lie.

By the time Dönitz got enough subs built to cause havoc in the Atlantic, the USA was producing transport ships at a rate of ten for every one the U-boats sank. Yes, England and Europe were under duress, but Germany never ruled the seas—only made things rough in *only* the Atlantic for a while. This is the first lie, and this is not history. How do I know? I was there.

Later in the show, the effort is used to make a (dubious) connection between Dönitz navy, the Enigma machine, and man's DNA in code and binary language. Once again, very fancy computer graphics are used to confuse us. Man's DNA and Enigma are in no way similar. The Enigma is a machine; man is sentient.

The narrator then tries (vainly) to connect Stephan J. Gould's hopeful monster theory of evolution, Darwin's evolution theory and enigma codes, and throwing in some more computer graphics and binary language.

This schnozzle starts with an ocean worm looking much like a centipede you might find under a rock in your garden; with more computer graphics, the "link" is made to eels, fish, sea mammals, birds, and eventually the cerebral cortex of man. Anyone who knows the slightest about genetics knows that breeding outside any kind is impossible—even for evolution. No matter how many billion years is added to the equation. I refer here again to museums worldwide. Museums have bones by the millions, but not a single transitional form.

The narrator starts his evolutionary escapade with a worm. This is curious, because Darwin's theory starts with some polypeptides coming together in some primordial soup to form an amoeba. Don't know where, don't know when. It just happened sometime after the big bang. But how did this "life" arise anyway. The heat produced by the big bang killed any life present according to Pasteur, and life does *not* come from nonlife. Never did, never will. Darwin would be turning over in his grave if he ever saw this show. According to Charles, life made a slow progress upward, not jumping from one species as shown in this comedy.

Big History is beautifully produced but gets the binary code connection all wrong. As an example of genetics moving backward, *not* forward, I present myself. I have a form of MS called cerebellar ataxia type 6. I have specialist reports on my condition after three and a half years' testing. (It's all in black and white.) The name designates the progressive nature of the condition. It does nothing whatsoever to offer any solution. I am a number 6. There are many other variants, up to twenty-four I know of. My condition is worsening, not getting better, as Darwin would suggest.

I make the suggestion that the experts in genetics that put this farce together spend more time trying to find a cure for me and many, many others around the country and the world. MS does not have a cure either, and these DNA and genetics "experts" on the National Geographic Channel are wasting their time trying to prove an unprovable theory instead of doing something useful.

When I was younger, I bred Appaloosa horses and studied genetics in an effort to find a solution to getting animals with the desired blanket pattern. I tried crossbreeding to Arabians. Horsemen and veterinarians are aware that the Arab breed has three lumbar vertebrae less than the Appaloosa or barb, and five less in the tail. An offspring of this outcross ends up with genes that do not send signals to the hind quarters, thus producing something called wobblers. The animal either dies or must be put down. So, you see, even crossbreeding within a kind is risky at best.

This national program will undoubtedly be replayed till it's worn out, but please be warned. Like Hitler said, "The bigger the lie, the more people will believe it."

By the way, Hitler lost WWII.

CHAPTER 12

Book of Joshua: A Fast-Paced Account of the Conquest of Canaan

IN VERSE 1, we have extraterrestrial involvement still, or again Joshua gets instructions from the Lord. The whole of the Fertile Crescent is defined as the Promised Land.

The harlot Rahab confirms that the Lord is God of heaven and earth beneath, and the inhabitants near Jordan are ready to run up the white flag. Joshua orders the Ark of the Covenant across the Jordan. Remember, the Jordan back then was a powerful river, not the shallow polluted trickle it is today. The waters near Jericho stood up in a heap, and the ark crossed on dry land.

We see now another extraterrestrial event. At the end of chapter 5, Joshua comes face-to-face with a man, an angel with a drawn sword, who identifies himself as the commander of the Lord's army. Instructions are given for Joshua's army to march around the city, once only for seven days in a row, blowing rams' horns and trumpets. On the seventh day, they must march around Jericho seven times; and at the end of marching and blowing rams' horns and trumpets, the whole congregation is to let out a shout at the top of their lungs, and the walls of Jericho will fall flat.

What's going on here? First is the noise of rams' horns and trumpets. This tells me that some kind of cadence is being set up to weaken the walls with sound-wave vibrations. An instrument, one string in between two others that are plucked, will set up sympathetic vibrations and start to vibrate of its own accord, without being touched. Somehow, the rams' horns and trumpets on either side of the city walls started a similar sympathetic vibration in the stonework. The vibrations were so great that on the seventh day, the walls could not resist the extra vibrations caused by a multitude of people shouting. This effect would have been more acute if the walls had any baked-brick areas incorporated in them. Remember the Pyramids; they have resonance granite blocks incorporated in them, like in your crystal-movement watch.

Every inhabitant in the city was killed, including livestock—except Rahab. The evil Canaanites were destroyed because they consistently did evil before the Lord, and God abhors evil.

On to chapter 10, Joshua continues to Ai and defeats it, then to Jerusalem and a combined force with Gibeon. They are routed, and the Lord finishes them with large hailstones in a nearby desert no less. During this rout of Gibeon, the sun and moon both stand still in the heavens for about a twenty-four-hour period while the battle rages.

This is truly an extraterrestrial happening—the earth standing still on its axis. The earth was not changing polarity or rotation. It went down in its normal manner when the Israelites had the victory. The sun and moon stood still for twenty-four hours; this indicate that a day is still a day and not a prolonged thousand-year period as some indicate happened during the Creation in Genesis. A day is always a day.

Joshua then conquers the giants (Anakim) in the mountains of Judah and Hebron. The only giants remaining were in Gaza in Gath and Ashdod. Joshua conquers all the lands at the east end of the Mediterranean. But where did the angel go?

Apparently, he seems to be acting as a supreme general, similar to Eisenhower on D-day. Orders are given to Joshua on how to survey and divide the land.

The giants in the Gaza area and the Philistines in the area bordering Egypt seemed to have posed a serious threat. They had technology superior to the Israelites', in particular, iron chariots and a force of Nephilim as mercenaries.

Because of the reluctance of the Israelites to attack the Gaza area, and the failing health of Joshua, this conquest was put on hold. Joshua died and was buried in Ephraim; the bones of Joseph were reburied nearby.

CHAPTER 13

AT THE END of the book of Joshua, we see the Israelites promising to follow their God and his statutes. They do this until the elders giving guidance to Joshua died. The Israelites started *backsliding* again. In the meantime, Judah attacked Gaza and surrounding lands and the remaining sons of Anak—except Goliath of Gath and his brothers.

Gath has been excavated and the Anak brothers' beds are more than nine feet long—big guys—but the bigger they are, the harder they fall.

At this time, we are told of the incomplete conquest of the Promised Land. The Lord came to an Israelite council at Bochim and told them in no uncertain terms of his dissatisfaction. The promise was that the remaining unconquered people would be "a thorn in the sides of Israel" and a snare (nothing but trouble). The area spoken of here is Gaza and East Egypt. This is the main land controlled by the Muslim Brotherhood, or Hamas today. The nation is not yet under a king. Judges are in office to lead and guide in war and dispense justice locally.

These Judges are Othniel, Ehud, Shamgar, Deborah, Barak, Gideon, Abimelech, Tola, Jair, Jephthah, Ibzan, Elon, Abdon, and Samson. All these judges play some part in keeping the Israelites true to their Lord God. Gideon's encounter with an extraterrestrial happens in chapter 6. The angel of the Lord appears again and tells Gideon that the Midianites will not prevail. Gideon wins and proceeds to rip down the Baal idols in Midian.

The Midianites aren't done. Gideon summons mercenaries but still doesn't think he has a chance. He asks God for a sign. A fleece is dry one morning, and all the ground is laden with dew. The following morning, the reverse is true. Now any of you who spends time camping will know that this is an impossibility, right? Well, in this case, I can't think of any logical explanation except an extraterrestrial occurrence. Gideon goes on to defeat the Midianite horde with only three hundred men.

Gideon dies, and Israel goes back to worshiping Baal and Asherah idols. Asherah poles are totems decorated with all sorts of regalia and often precious metals and jewels.

It seems that grapes play an important role in the Old (and New) Testaments. Chapter 9:13 mentions that new wine cheers both God and men. Unfermented wine "cheers" no one. In verse 27, Gaal made wine "and made merry." Unfermented wine makes no man merry. First thing Noah did after disembarking was to get drunk. Wine and strong drinks are to be avoided, because drunkenness is a *pit* you can fall into. However, small amounts of wine are good for the digestion and make you warm inside. Besides, moderate drinkers outlive teetotalers, and Jesus tells us to take a little wine for medicinal purposes.

It seems like tending vineyards was "women's" work at this time. We see the sons of Benjamin given special privileges in the vineyards. This is not the norm in a civilized society, and the judges did not have enough wherewithal to do differently.

Now we see the need for a ruler with power (a king) other than God, but first a love story.

Ruth is the kind of woman every man should have for a wife. Boaz was a lucky man, and Ruth was a lucky woman. There is no specific extraterrestrial event in this book, unless you count their meeting as an act of the Lord.

Samson is the last really important judge. He has an extraterrestrial encounter and gains great strength by being true to his vows. This isn't going to happen to people in today's age, but I urge you to read his story in toto. Samuel sees a king enter King Saul.

CHAPTER 14

S AMUEL RECOUNTS HOW the Israelites backslid into idolatry again and why a king was needed to keep order in an ever-increasing population growth. At first, Saul was an obvious choice, but he ultimately disobeyed the commands of God that got him the position in the first place. Then David replaced him. Israel was at a religious low point when Saul came to power. There were a few righteous, who worshiped at Shiloah, where God's presence abided in the Tabernacle. The Ark of the Covenant was briefly captured by the Philistines until David recaptured it and returned it to Jerusalem.

It seems that the Judges abused their power, and the people demanded a king. Enters Samuel. The book of Samuel opens with Samuel's genealogy. His father had two wives. This was an accepted custom of the time. Samuel's father took a second wife because his first wife was barren. God's law forbade polygamy and later gave the tragic results of marrying many wives.

So Hannah was barren and prayed for an extraterrestrial intervention that she should have a son. The priest Eli also blessed that her petition be granted.

Samuel is born. Hannah's prayer is one that we all need to emulate (chapter 2). In it, she acknowledges that the coming Christ is the savior. This, many hundreds of years before the fact, she acknowledges: Christ is the rock of our salvation (not

Peter). She knows that the dead sleep in the dust and are raised up (verses 6–8) and are not in heaven.

All in all, this prayer is from an astonishingly literate woman for the time. The priest Eli's sons were wicked, so he adopted Samuel in their place. Because of Hanna's faithfulness, God blessed her with five more children.

Samuel is called *audibly* in an extraterrestrial manner at bedtime late one evening. God, the extraterrestrial, tells Samuel that Eli will be punished because he had allowed his sons to become vile and did not restrain or reprimand them. Eli dies, and Samuel takes his place, as predicted by an unnamed prophet in chapter 2:27.

The Philistines attack and capture the ark and take it and put it in the temple of Dagon at Ashdod. The first morning, the huge statue of Dagon has fallen flat on its face, smashed (it was never fixed). From Gath to Ekron, it was the same problem. At Ashdod, a vile epidemic breaks out—tumors and sores. The ark is taken to Gath, and the same epidemic follows. They finally get the message, and the ark is returned to Israel—no more epidemic. There was a large number of Philistines that accompanied the ark back to Israel. When the ark was secure again, the Lord smote (struck) fifty thousand Israelites down for their transgressions. Was this something like we see in *Raiders of the Lost Ark*? With fire coming from the ark and consuming the Nazis possibly?

Even after this event, the Israelites are still discontent and demanding a king. God tells Samuel not to be discouraged, because it's God they have rejected, not Samuel. Saul is chosen because he was tall and handsome (don't judge a book by its cover). Saul immediately becomes a false prophet. See chapter 10:9–14. Saul wavers between sinning and a desire to serve God. In the end, sin wins out, and Saul dies a tragic death, as we will see.

Samuel admonishes the Israelites for demanding a king and calls down thunder and rain (in torrents) to prove his point.

In the next few chapters, the Lord saves Saul and Jonathan on numerous occasions in battles they had no right winning. And see here, it's the Philistines from the area around Gaza that cause the problems, the same Philistines that were not exterminated by Joshua when they had the chance. These same Philistines continue today as Palestinians, Hamas, and to a lesser degree, the Muslim Brotherhood and Isis.

During all this warring, we finally see Saul getting pushed more and more into a military position, from which it seems there is no escape. He runs out of options and loses faith in his own abilities as commander. Saul makes a fateful choice to contact extraterrestrial help out of the dilemma. Enter the medium, the witch of Endor. Saul had previously banished witches, wizards, necromancers, mediums, etc., from Israel. Now he sees an opportunity to get the upper hand on the enemies.

Bad Choice

In disguise, Saul travels to Endor for what some theologians call a séance. That's what I suspect it was supposed to be. But it is *not* a séance. These are the people that are supposed to be able to contact the "spirits of the dead." I urge you to read the intervening chapters to get a complete picture of Saul's interactions with David. There was a time here when we see the "feet of clay" of David the king. David made a lot of errors in his life, but unlike Saul, he recognized his errors and recanted and asked the Lord's forgiveness. Saul did not. By the time Saul gets to Endor, Samuel is long dead. The young witch has "powers," all right, but is ignorant of their source (possibly?). She recognizes Saul and denies her powers. Saul promises that no harm will come to her.

One thing I know about séances is that the medium (witch) is in control of the proceedings. She was not. She asks for the name of the person's spirit that she should bring up. Before Saul can tell her, God brings up Samuel. This was nothing she had any control over. Her reactions are explanation enough. She screamed and shrank into a corner. The witch saw the apparition. Saul did not. At this point, Samuel's presence came out of the earth, not descend from heaven. The apparition Samuel then speaks to Saul audibly and says, "Why have you disturbed me?"—just what someone is likely to say when woken in the middle of the night's sleep.

Samuel tells Saul that he, his sons, and a host of Israelites will die the next day. Samuel also says that they "will be with me." This statement simply means they will be dead, in the earth, awaiting the second resurrection, as opposed to the pretribulation rapture of the dead, before the Second Coming.

So the medium was shown up for what she was, a phony, a charlatan? Not really, mediums have certain "powers" but not to bring up the spirits of any dead people. As we will see in Ecclesiastes 9, Solomon, David's son (second wisest man to ever live), tells us that the dead do not, nor cannot, have anything to do with the living.

This being the case, what, or who, is it that mediums contact? They themselves don't know. It is the demon spirits of those "fallen angels" we met in Genesis. Remember those "sons of God" that intermarried with mortals? These beings do not die (yet) unfortunately, and they vex naive people (silly women) and, unfortunately, men calling themselves wizards and warlocks or shaman or "gifted" psychic.

Samuel records the tragic end of Saul and his sons. The audible conversation between Samuel and Saul is extraterrestrial. Samuel's chitchat with Saul is not heard by anyone other than Saul. As far as we know, the witch was still cowering in the corner.

The term "bringing up" can only be explained by God's intervention and producing the apparition. From what Samuel says, he is in the *grave*—not in heaven as some believe. If he was brought down he would have used the term "brought down." No? I think so.

So Samuel speaks and is heard and seen by Saul (and whoever recorded the event, probably one of Saul's attendants). The witch comes to her senses and makes Saul and his servants a big meal, and they depart, distressed. The prophecy comes true. Saul dies the next day (by suicide), and David takes over as king.

One of David's first encounters with an extraterrestrial context is his conversation with Achish. Achish is the name of the Philistine ruler of Gath, where David had fled to hide from Saul. But here, they are familiar with angels, or so it would seem. Just how they are familiar with this sort of extraterrestrial is yet to be seen.

David's first wives, Ahinoam and Abigail, are taken captive, and David asks the Lord what will happen if he pursues the captors. It is not explained how the messages are given to God, or how any answer comes back. However, since David and the Israelites have the Ark of the Covenant in their possession, we must assume that the ark has some part to play here. Again, I mention that in the '50s (I believe), students at John Hopkins University proceeded to make a replica of the ark. An exact copy had to be abandoned before completion, because of the electrostatic emanations. This indicates, to me, anyway, that God (Jehovah) can, and does, use his creation to communicate with us.

The accounts of the first part of Samuel were written by Samuel. Since Samuel dies early in the first part of 1 Samuel, it is (rightly) assumed that the prophet Nathan completed the books, being an eyewitness to the life and happenings of David, etc.

The division of God's people happens, David over Judah and Ish-bosheth over Israel (all the rest). This leads to war between the two sides, with David the victor, as predicted. After all, David is God's anointed and in possession of extraterrestrial powers contained in the ark. It seems like David was a precursor of Alexander the Great, winning battles and conquering his enemies by the thousands.

David's actions with the women in his life are his own choice, and he is punished for them. David recants and is forgiven. There is the little excursion against Goliath of Gath. David had fled to Gath to hide from Saul. He was surely familiar with Goliath and family during this time, so meeting him in battle with the sling and stones was not as daunting as it might seem at first. David took extra stones in case he needed them, not because he might miss, but as defense against Goliath's brothers, who would surely wish to avenge their brother's death. This is not recorded.

The book of Second Samuel ends with an extraterrestrial event, when God removes a plague from Israel that David had brought on Israel for his sins. It seems that God was displeased that David had sinned and sent an "angel" to destroy Jerusalem. Apparently, this extraterrestrial being is very real and has extraordinary powers. Thousands died from an unspecified plague. Jerusalem was spared by extraterrestrial intervention. David builds an altar and offers a sacrifice that satisfies God as to his repentance, and the plague stops.

CHAPTER 15

THE COMMENTATOR OF my NKJV says, in the outline, that the (nonexistent) pre-Christian Septuagint originally combined First and Second Samuel and First and Second Kings together. At this point, I really wonder how this can be, the extant pre-Christian Septuagint being a fable invented by Origen. It may very well be possible this is so. However, to make this assumption based on nonexistent document is presumptive in the least.

I suggest that too much time is wasted in trying to determine authorship and dates. Instead, more time needs to be spent on accuracy and meaning of the message contained. Since most scholars agree that God wrote the Bible through the actions of the Holy Spirit, why spend so much time trying to get into the ink wells of the writers?

The book of Kings ends with David charging Solomon to keep God's statutes. David dies and sleeps with his fathers. The text does *not* say David goes to heaven, this being a pagan idea started by Semiramis in Babylon. David has not risen to the heavens. Acts 2:34 tells us David is in his grave awaiting the Second Coming. Believe it or not, it's up to you.

One of Solomon's first political acts was the wise move to make a treaty with the Pharaoh of Egypt. He sealed the pact by taking as wife one of Pharaoh's daughters. The Pharaoh at the time was probably Ramses II. He had upwards of one hundred sons and daughters and was, I expect, glad to reduce his responsibilities somewhat. Free from the possibility of wars, Solomon's reign was prosperous. Solomon completes his own extravagant house fit for the daughter of Ramses and others, and he completes the temple in Jerusalem. It seems Solomon now has access to this direct link of communication with God through the ark. God, the extraterrestrial, promises to perform his word if Solomon remains true to the covenant God made with David.

Solomon hires Hiram Abiff to do all the brass and cedar work in the temple. Hiram Abiff was a Phoenician, from Tyre. He was hired for his prowess, not for his religious background. He was married to a Jewish woman and claimed Jewish heritage through her. Herein lies a problem. Freemasonry claims its roots go back to Solomon's temple. The claim being that Phoenician "secrets" and temple building details are incorporated in the temple itself. Apart from Hiram Abiff's Phoenician background, the so-called Phoenician secrets are the only direct connection that Freemasonry has to Solomon's temple. The so-called secrets are pagan and not from Solomon or God. So Freemasonry is based directly on pagan rituals and not from God. Freemasonic claims to godhood also fall short. The god of Freemasonry is an unnamed god. The Hebrew god has a name—*Yhwh* ("I am")—and incarnates himself as Jesus later in the book.

Solomon gives God the glory, not GAOTU or Jahbulon, the god of the Freemasons. The father of modern Freemasonry goes one step further and calls Lucifer god in one of his speeches to the meetings of the grand councils its history, so any connection as to origins is dubious, to say the least. It's unbelievable just how far the truth can be misconstrued. Whew.

When the temple is finished, God, the extraterrestrial, appears to Solomon again by night. This could be a dream, but I suspect it to be verbal communications, as with Samuel, by night. God tells Solomon that he will keep his word to prosper Solomon's reign and the Israelites, if Solomon keeps his end of the bargain. Solomon is terribly human and finds too many women attractive. Just as today, when men everywhere are marinating in porn, Solomon does not hold up his end (chapter 11). When Solomon starts turning to the gods of his foreign wives, Pharaoh, probably Shishak, makes an alliance with Hadad.

Solomon worshiped Ashtoreth, Milcom, Chemosh, and other gods requiring the burning of incense. God visits Solomon in his depravity and tells him that the kingdom will fall to his servant. Solomon reigns forty years and dies. He also sleeps with his fathers.

Rehoboam becomes king and increases the people's workload—he increases their taxes. First Kings 13 tells of King Jeroboam harassing a prophet of God and his hand and arm becoming "withered" and immobile. All I can say here is, "Don't mess with God, you can't win." Jeroboam's altar is destroyed, and his arm withers. His arm is restored by a passing prophet, but the prophet is seduced by a liar to make the real prophet transgress his orders from God. He succumbs to the lie and is killed by a lion.

Now, all this is very good and shows some extraterrestrial involvement. But what is the purpose but to get across the point: we must obey God in all things, keep our word, be steadfast in what we know to be the truth.

Here follows a succession of kings, with some being good and some bad: Asa is one good king, who, among other things, cut down an obscene totem of Asherah and removed his grandmother from being queen mother because she had made it. Asa also removed many other idols and totems from Judah, back and forth till we get to chapter 17. Ahab reigns in Israel and marries Jezebel. Ahab makes many idols to Baal.

Enter Elijah, probably the best-known prophet. His story abounds with extraterrestrial happenings, so let's consider them in more detail.

CHAPTER 16

ELIJAH GETS OFF on the wrong foot immediately with Ahab and Jezebel. He declares drought because of their worship of Baal. After doing so, God tells him to hide by the brook Cherith, where ravens will feed him. The order to hide is reasonable due to the explosive temperament of Ahab's wife. The name Jezebel is renounced for infamy, even today. Eventually, this Jordan tributary dried up due to the drought.

Elijah is told to go to Zeraphath, a nearby town, and meet a widow for shelter. He does, and because he is thirsty, not having drunk for some time, he looks like a "likely case," so she invites him into her house. The feeding of Elijah by ravens is obviously an act of an extraterrestrial. Who commands ravens to feed anyone? They are notorious scavengers. This has to be extraordinary.

The widow's son dies, and the widow blames Elijah. Why? I'm not sure. In any case, Elijah restores the boy, and his soul is restored and he becomes alive again. Notice, the boy does not say one word about having to return from heaven (or paradise or Valhalla or nirvana or the happy hunting grounds or anywhere else). Simple reason is, because his soul didn't have any consciousness. Like David, Solomon, and others, he was sleeping with his fathers. In this case, he didn't sleep very long, because Elijah raised him back to life.

Elijah is told to pay a visit to Ahab, and the drought will end. Jezebel is happily killing God's prophets, but Obadiah has hidden some, like Schindler did with Jews in Nazi Germany in WWII. Elijah is fed up with Ahab's apostasy and worship of Baal that he calls for a showdown on Mount Carmel. For whatever reason, Ahab assembles 450 prophets of Baal and 400 of Asherah. Here, we see a great gathering of people on the mountain, something like the FIFA World Cup. This "showdown" comes about because Ahab accuses Elijah of being a thorn in the side of Baal worshipers everywhere, and I'm sure, with Jezebel's urging, it seems like a good way to shut him up once and for all.

Apparently, Jezebel had managed to get rid of all God's prophets but this one. Through extraterrestrial providence, Elijah escaped, only to end up alone as God's voice on the mountain. The lines in the sand are drawn; Elijah lays fair ground rules, same for him and the 850 prophets against him. They are to make two wooden pyres and put a bullock on each. Then he tells them to douse the pyres with water so they are soaked. Balaam's and Asherah's priests go through all kinds of incantations, to no avail. Elijah mocks them, saying, "Shout louder, possibly he is asleep." One from the original texts says that Elijah mocks them by saying, "Call louder, possibly he has gone out for a piss."

Is this irreverent? Not really. Elijah knew what he was saying. More believers should be so bold. The one that calls fire from heaven to burn their pyre is the prophet of the true God. The false prophets of Baal and Asherah fail miserably. Elijah's pyre is burned when the extraterrestrial God of creation burns not only his pyre but Balaam's also. All the people present, and there seems to have been many, seize and kill the false prophets. Jezebel is in a rage.

Ahab goes with Elijah to the top of Mount Carmel and is told seven times to look out to sea to see something. The seventh time, Ahab sees the hand of God in the form of a cloud. This is the drought being broken. And it starts to pour.

Jezebel swears to kill Elijah within twenty-four hours. Elijah flees, and while resting under a broom tree, which is abundant in Israel, an extraterrestrial touches him. Jesus, as the angel of the Lord in preincarnate form, bakes Elijah "some cake." Elijah is aroused from sleep twice to eat and drink for his coming trek. Elijah goes forty days and nights on the strength of these two meals. Grocery stores wouldn't get rich from this guy.

Elijah makes it to a cave on Mount Horeb, where he gets another extraterrestrial visit. Elijah is to go to Damascus and anoint three men, two as kings and Elisha as his successor. Elijah now has an assistant (disciple).

The text takes an excursion here to tell of succeeding kings and how they slept with their fathers when they died. It seems that Baal worship became rampant again in this period, except Jehoshaphat, who was God fearing and built an extensive navy that sailed the world trading for all manners of goods to prosper Israel. Then came Ahaziah, who went and spoiled things again.

All these kings died and slept with their fathers. I think the text is trying to tell us something here.

CHAPTER 17

S ECOND KINGS CONTINUES with the angel of
the Lord speaking to Elijah. Here again, it is generally
considered by most experts that an angel of the lord is an
extraterrestrial messenger, as distinct from God incarnate. The
angel of the Lord is Jesus in preincarnate form. Here, the angel
tells Elijah to warn Ahaziah of his impending death. Ahaziah
sends for Elijah to face him directly. On two occasions, the
fifty-man posse is burned by "fire from God." The third time,
God, the extraterrestrial, allows Elijah to go with them. They
must have been a terrified bunch.

Ahaziah's other deeds are recorded in Chronicles, which we
will get to. Soon Ahaziah is on his deathbed, as Elijah had said,
and he dies.

Second Kings 2 gives an extraordinary account of Elijah
being transported directly to heaven without seeing death. He is
taken up in a whirlwind. My Bible commentary says absolutely
nothing as a possible explanation of this event. This leaves me
even more interested as to what happened. Whirlwinds on earth
nowadays are tornadoes. But Elijah is not reported as being
dumped somewhere nearby, all mangled up. We must assume
that an extraordinary extraterrestrial event happened.

Elijah is one of up to six special "men of God" that went
directly to heaven by similar means. So where did he go? Not
to a spaceship, because the texts say he went to heaven, which,

to the best of my knowledge, is another dimension, probably timeless as we know it. See chapter 2:10. The whirlwind came in conjunction with a fiery chariot with fiery horses. Now here we have something to work with. While Elijah was transported in the whirlwind, the fiery chariot hid Elijah from Elisha's sight.

What could a fiery chariot be described as in 2014 language? The TV is replete with UFO and ancient astronaut programs. I cannot totally disagree that fiery chariot and fiery horses certainly do seem possible. Here we must consider other possibilities. We know that God is omnipresent, but what about angels, both good angels that are messengers of God and fallen angels that rebelled against God and got kicked out of heaven? This event is explained briefly in Isaiah 14.

Elijah is gone, and Elisha takes his place. Elijah was the first of two men that were taken to heaven directly without seeing death. The other was Enoch, who went second class (without reference to fiery horses). There were four others (only) that died and went to heaven, the first being Moses. The rest of us have to wait till Christ's return and the dead saints are raised.

Elisha is a good disciple of Elijah. He is taken in by a local widow and repays her by giving her a jar of oil that is never emptied during her lifetime. He also raises a man from the dead. Elisha cures Naaman's leprosy (chapter 5:7). It seems Elisha was a man of means. One day, while riding in his chariot, he is approached by a greedy servant of Naaman. He asks for two talents of silver (approximately fifty-seven pounds). The thief is found out, and Naaman's leprosy is transferred to the wicked servant *and his descendants.*

Elisha helps some men build a house near the Jordan. An ax breaks, and the axe head flies into the river. Elisha takes a stick and causes the axe head to "float" to the surface.

A Syrian army lays siege to the city of Dothan (Genesis 37:17), and here the attacking force is great, and Elisha's servant is troubled that they will all be killed. Elisha prays that his servant's eyes be opened. The servant sees the attacking army surrounded by many (uncounted) fiery chariots and fiery horses; ever hear of *them* before?

Is this just another close encounter? There's certainly room for thought here. The resulting attack by the Syrian army results in a mass blindness of the attacking force. Elisha and the Israeli king make a pact to give them a banquet. Their blindness is removed, they have the banquet, and they return to Syria and do not attack Israel again. Possibly a lesson could be learned here, and tried by NATO or the UN?

Where has Jezebel been for the last fourteen years? She kept her evil ways, always harassing God's prophets. Her luck finally runs out (chapter 9). Jezebel is looking from a window in the city wall, accusing one of God's prophets (Jehu) of murder (a false accusation). He tells two of her servants to throw her out the window. They do. She dies. Horses passing trampled her. The prophet Jehu tells his servants to go and give her a decent burial because she is (was) a king's daughter. When they get to the city gates, all they find is her skull and her hands.

This is a fulfilled prophecy of Elijah: "Dogs will eat her flesh and her other remains will be refuse on the land."

Some might think this a terrible end for anyone, let alone a princess. But she was more than an annoyance to God and his servants all her life. Whose side are you on?

We aren't told a lot about this "war" in heaven. We must accept it happened some time during the Creation. That's fine, but since these good and "bad" angels are not omnipresent, how do they get around, and where are they hiding? Again, are they hiding, or are they walking the earth as men and women? They must be able to transmute matter as Jannes and Jambres did for Pharaoh. But God is not an ancient astronaut.

CHAPTER 18

MORE KINGS OF Judah and Israel come and go and sleep with their fathers. Elisha dies. The account of his death is interesting. Joash is king. On Elisha's deathbed, Elisha tells Joash to bring a bow and arrows. With Joash's aid, Elisha fires an arrow out the window. Joash is told to strike the ground, and he does so, three times. This is symbolic of the number of times he will have success against the Syrians.

Joash has the successes prophesied but ultimately does not utterly destroy the Syrians as he should have done if he had struck the ground five or six times. The Syrians attack Israel to this day because of Joash's error.

Elisha died and was buried, but before the grave was filled in, a raiding band attacked a nearby burial, interrupting it, and the corps was thrown into Elisha's grave. The corps became alive. End of story. Some may wish to say this was not an extraterrestrial, or miraculous, happening. However, people back then were acutely aware of what constituted life and death. There were so many wars and battles going on. There did not seem to be much of a feeling for the sanctity of life as we have written in our laws today. That said, our laws do seem to be reversing. Witness the riots in United States cities—it's scary to see murder happen in front of the TV cameras. And justice is not happening.

But this corps came alive as recorded by witnesses. There is a brief period when no prophets of note are in Israel or Judah.

Many kings come and go and sleep with their fathers. Along comes Isaiah, who assures deliverance from the Assyrians. This is recorded at the end of 2 Kings 19, where, in verse 35, it is the angel of the Lord that kills 185,000 Assyrians.

King Sennacherib returns home and is assassinated while worshiping his pagan god, by two of his sons no less. And they flee to southern Turkey. A couple more kings are recorded, and we come to Jehoiakim. Pharaoh Necho set up Jehoiakim in place of Jehoahaz.

It seems that poor old Judah and Israel always get caught in the middle. Necho had to cross Judah and Israel to get to the main adversary, the Assyrians. To get to his destination, he had triremes built at the Red Sea. The remnants, windlasses (winches for hauling heavy weights), still remain as evidence of this campaign. The campaign is recorded in Herodotus histories and the book of Chronicles. This endeavor happened in 600 BC. The triremes were built on the Red Sea and sailed around Africa to the Nile Delta. Necho was in the process of digging the equivalent of the Suez Canal.

I guess we could call it the Necho Canal. The project was put on hold. Necho won some skirmishes but ultimately lost control of all lands from the Nile to Babylon—as predicted.

Jerusalem and the Promised Land are still caught in the middle. Jerusalem is captured, and all the works of brass, gold, and silver items made by Hiram Abiff for Solomon's temple were cut up as loot, and the majority of the people were taken captive to Babylon.

What about Pharaoh Necho? He declines as a minor pharaoh (a "looser" as history records him). This is the beginning of the end for Egypt's greatness. Roughly three hundred years later, Alexander the Great comes on the scene. A few years later, another raid is made into Judah, and the rest of the Jews are taken into captivity. Once again a captive, Jehoiakim, becomes a king's right-hand man.

CHAPTER 19

CHRONICLES IS WRITTEN by Ezra about the middle of the third century BC.

Hannibal is crossing the Alps, the Chinese terracotta army is constructed, Ptolemy (Soter, of Philadelphus?) is in power in Egypt, Alexander is dead, the Roman state is beginning to emerge, Carthage is razed—but no historical record of the Septuagint so far. Is this an oversight by history, and is this where tradition takes over?

Never mind, we'll cover this later (again). However, it is odd that Ezra, or the author of Chronicles, does *not* mention such a stupendous undertaking. Chronicles gives Adam's genealogy (again). The genealogies of many notable Hebrew families is also given even to the specific tribes.

Let's deal with Levitical "duties" for a minute. The duties were as guards of the treasury, and as such, this included guarding the ark and the books of the law (Pentateuch). No other tribe had these rights per David. Any copying of these writings was strictly controlled by these men. For tradition to say that six men from each tribe went to Alexandria under Ptolemy's encouragement to translate these writings is preposterous. Firstly, the writings would *not* have been allowed past the Tabernacle's front tent flap. This means that if these men *did* go to Alexandria to do this work, they each would have had to have memorized the entire works. This is as much an impossibility of Origen memorizing the finished Greek translation. But this is the story presented by tradition, not history.

As tradition goes, each scholar, six from each tribe, was sequestered to his own cubicle for the duration. And wonder of wonders. Every man came up with a perfect rendering in Greek. Believe this if you will, but I have some swampland up north I want you to see. Basically, the book of Chronicles recaps a lot of what we have covered. If I come up with anything extraterrestrial, I will cover it in the next chapter.

Chronicles 24 is interesting. Specific mention is made of the adversary by name—Satan. Apparently God condoned this action against David. A census was taken. The final number was roughly the same as when Moses led them out of Egypt. This is soon followed with David visibly seeing an angel hovering over Jerusalem with a drawn sword.

No fiery chariot or fiery horses are mentioned. No whirlwind accompanies the vision. There is here a duplication of what we find in Kings, until 2 Chronicles 14. Even though the Ethiopian queen of Sheba found favor at her visit to Solomon's court, things were not entirely OK in Ethiopia. An Ethiopian army, possibly mercenaries allied to Pharaoh Shishak, came against King Asa. One million men and three hundred chariots were a sizable mercenary army. The Lord struck the Ethiopians. It doesn't say how or for how long, but they fled.

From what I have learned about Ethiopians during the Zulu wars and similar, they drugged themselves before going into battle. It wouldn't surprise me to find that in this case, they "overdosed," or was it an intervention by extraterrestrial powers?

The Ethiopian army was allied with Arabians (chapter 21:16 and 22:1). So it would seem the term *Arabian* was not first introduced into the language by T. E. Lawrence.

Things do not go well for Ahaziah, because of this association and the bad advice of his mother, and he slept with his fathers. Priestly power and control wanes until Jehoiada tears down the idols of Baal in Judah and restores the gatekeeper role to the Levites.

All in all, the book of Chronicles retells the ups and downs during the rule of Jewish kings, with God more or less keeping out of it all most of the time. This book ends with an extraordinary extraterrestrial event. King Cyrus of Persia proclaims the Lord God of Israel and Judah is the true God. Cyrus builds a house of worship for God in Jerusalem. This is history, not tradition.

Under Cyrus, the captive Jews and other conquered people were freed to return to their homelands. Since the Jews had no idols to take back with them, the ark and temple artifacts were returned too.

On to Ezra.

By this time, I think you can see that God has not given up on his chosen. He speaks and acts through godly men on his behalf. Nehemiah is still in Persia with Artaxerxes ruling. He requests permission to go to Jerusalem. The language used indicates he has some "pull" at court. He gets permission (written orders) and goes to Jerusalem, where he sets to building the walls.

It seems the fair weights and measures act did not extend to Jerusalem. The leaders were notorious "thieves," and when a famine struck the area (again), the people had no way to survive with no money. Nehemiah cancels all debts to solve the problem. I guess the nobles didn't like this idea because they conspire to kill the prophet.

A long genealogy follows regarding the families who resettle inside the city, certainly enough to defend it against Saladin when the time comes.

One of Hollywood's better achievements is depicted in *The Kingdom of Heaven*, with Eva Green, Orlando Bloom, and Liam Neeson. Worth a watch.

Jerusalem is resettled and thriving, roughly half the size of the town I live. Ezra is a contemporary and aids Nehemiah in getting things back to normality. By the end of the book of Nehemiah, all traces of pagan worship are nonexistent in Jerusalem; even the Levites who had erred were gone.

Esther

Theories dating the book of Esther are the Septuagint and Josephus. Since there is no pre-Christian Septuagint, as previously explained at length, I must assume Josephus dates are correct. Esther became queen to Ahasuerus of Persia in 404 BC. The book itself nowhere mentions God, the temple, law of Moses, Palestine, or Jerusalem. This is the most UN Jewish or

UN Christian book in the Bible. Some wonder why it is even there.

Until we read and find the book written for Jews of the early Diaspora, the time between the destruction of Jerusalem around 550 BC to the destruction of Jerusalem by the Romans in 70 AD. We see the feast of Purim instituted and an excellent set of ethical rules laid out for captured people dealing with anti-Semitism.

Since there are no extraterrestrial events recorded, we move from one book with none other than Job, where there are many.

CHAPTER 20

FURTHER ON THE subject of, is God an ancient astronaut? The answer for Erich von Däniken and his "ancient astronaut" theorists is N.D. Erich has not read the Bible thoroughly, or in context. If he had, he would know God is omnipresent and does *not* need a spaceship to get around. On the other hand, angels of God and the fallen angels (demons) are not God, or gods, and do need some sort of what we might term extraterrestrial transportation. In referring to God the Creator as extraterrestrial, I only do this to relate the fact that both God the Creator and the angels are not from earth or any other planet. They have the ability to interact with humans by entering this reality by choice at any time; angels come and go, and God does the same. Difference being, God is everywhere at once (according to what he says about himself in the texts). On the other hand, angels need to transport themselves in other ways.

There are many instances of seemingly extraterrestrial activity recorded in the Bible, and more of these will be mentioned later. In today's world, there are too many sightings and close encounters to be ignored (Hollywood excluded). My own experiences with spacecraft are nominal compared to some, but worth recounting here.

One night, returning home late from work, I stopped the car. I pulled over to get a glimpse of the newly completed CN

Tower and the recently completed Channel 9 antenna. I was a good deal away from Toronto, on the Aurora side road. The night was clear and still, and the city lights were amazing. I concentrated on the sights and suddenly realized there was a "light" moving between the two towers I had stopped to see. The light was moving from close to the CN Tower and quickly shot over to near the antenna. This happened a few times, then it came back to the antenna, sped straight up, and disappeared at about a thousand feet.

The other occasion, I was on my back porch with my daughter. We decided to look for satellites before her bedtime (any excuse to stay up a little later). We got small lounge chairs in order not to strain our necks. I had two pairs of binoculars. Two satellites were seen. I suggested she could head to bed after one circled the earth and made another pass. As it came into view, we saw what appeared to be a second-magnitude star directly in the line of sight move. We concentrated on it as it quickly sped in the direction of the satellite, but seemingly a good distance behind. The object at first seemed to be interested in the satellite but suddenly made a reverse turn away. The angle of the turn was about twenty degrees, made at great undetermined speed, without slowing down. The "thing" disappeared off the horizon, to the south.

There have been many TV shows recently exploring this type of phenomenon, and no, I (we) have never been abducted. Nothing conclusive has been determined for lack of physical evidence. But there is definitely something going on that we cannot explain. It is therefore not too smart to discount the Bible accounts as fables. These people thousands of years ago were obviously seeing the same things we are seeing but described them in five-thousand-year-old language, with references from their reality.

So was Elijah's "fiery chariot" a chariot with fiery horses? Or if he were living today, would he describe a space shuttle launch, or possibly a V-2 rocket or a flying saucer? Possibly a Concorde jet? Can we discount his description as fantasy? I think this would be presumptuous, to say the least.

Ever wonder why Project Blue Book was cancelled? We are told it was from lack of funding or inconclusive reporting. Really? Or possibly they got too close to the truth, and Area 51 and other secret sites really are run by aliens (fallen angels in disguise?). After all, if they really can transmute matter, who would know? Hiding in plain sight would be easy.

Sometime in the 1980s, I attended three series of lectures by Dr. Walter Martin. He was the founder of Christian Research Institute and the original Bible Answer Man. During the lectures, he said that he was part of the Project Blue Book team. At that time, he apparently had challenged Erich von Däniken, of "God as an ancient astronaut" theory, to a debate (discussion) in a public forum. Erich never did accept the "offer" (challenge).

CHAPTER 21

S OME SCHOLARS COUNT the book of Job to be the earliest book of the Old Testament. The author is unknown, and the writer is uncertain. The book was compiled somewhere near the end of the Iron Age, in Solomon's kingdom. Iron tools are mentioned, as well as mining, with all the accompanying duties inherent in mining. The "sons of God" are mentioned as "presenting" themselves before God. This can only take place in heaven, that other elevated dimension we mentioned previously. Satan and the rebels were definitely kicked out. As such, they were relegated to insignificance, with accompanying loss of influence and power. They still have access to God in this reduced capacity.

Satan and some of his assistants approach the throne in some sort of council chamber. God opens the discussion by asking Satan (Lucifer) what is his purpose in being there. My first question here is, where are the security guards, and how did Satan get past them? On further thought, was Satan deliberately allowed in? Possibly.

Satan answers that he "has been cruising the earth," obviously in disguise. Unlike Halloween night, when kids wear a red suit, pitchfork, and tail, Satan wears a business suit, or casuals, as the occasion calls for. Second Corinthians 11:13 tells this precisely—Satan and his demons (the biblical term for extraterrestrial cohorts) as being able to transmute matter in order to appear as anything and anyone they wish at will. The Greek word used here is *metaskenetzio*. This in no way indicates the putting on of a disguise, but rather the literal changing of the "substance" of matter. Some pastors insist this passage means the putting on of a disguise. It does not. The resulting transfer is accomplished by Satan, the shape-shifter. Or Satan the Comoloid? But he tells God that he has roamed the earth physically, or as someone (or thing) else. His purpose being to see how depraved or good men are. The book by C. S. Lewis *The Screwtape Letters* gives a fictional account of this kind of activity and would be a recommended read on the subject.

God asks Satan what he thinks of his servant Job. And the contest begins. Job's wealth is measured in cattle, and he is very well-off. With property and home and family, etc., God lets Satan test Job through many trials and loss of all his family and cattle. Job does not blame his loss on God and believes God is somehow testing him. When he loses his health through Satan's incredible insane test, his three best friends try to change his mind. The friends' good intentions go for nothing, and Job is eventually rewarded by God for his faithfulness. His health is restored, he remarries, and he ends up getting a new family and more livestock than before.

Satan is limited; he can only be in one place at one time. He must rely on his demon assistants for help. Making an observance here, many UFO sightings and extraterrestrial phenomenon are satanic. To say otherwise is to deny Albert Pike, Anton LaVey, Madame Blavatsky, and others who say this is so.

Just the other day, I was asked if I could explain some apparitions that happened in a friend's bedroom. There is more out there than meets the eye, for sure. Is it good, or adversarial? Can you rely on mediums like the Endor witch or mediums of any kind to tell you the "truth"?

Job comes through with flying colors, and God the Creator decides to give Job some congratulations and a pep talk. While we are flipping to chapter 26, where Job gets a chance to state his case for his steadfastness, we should pause at chapter 7:9–10. Job describes the "life of man" as a cloud (a wisp of smoke) that goes to the grave (when he dies) and does *not* rise to play a part on earth anymore. Again in chapter 14:11–15, once man dies, he's dead and has no part on anything that happens on earth, until Jesus returns. Solomon says exactly the same thing in Ecclesiastes 9.

This statement nullifies any activity of raising spirits from the dead at séances or any other time. Mediums that say they can raise the spirits of the dead are lying. The only spirits that are raised up are demonic apparitions sent by Satan to deceive. This also precludes any dead people from going to heaven before Christ's second coming (singular).

Job and Solomon both are telling us that the grave (earth) keeps our souls until the resurrection. It's only our life force (spirit), explained somewhat in chapter 32:8, that returns to God at death, and that's not the same. God will not release this life force until and unless he wants to at the resurrection of life, the first resurrection or the second resurrection of the dammed one thousand years later. Yes, there is extraterrestrial life, and the Creator God, Jehovah Elohim, has control (thank God).

In chapter 38, God speaks out of the whirlwind. Here we find that it was God that took Elijah—in the same whirlwind, I expect.

Now to Job's pep talk. The intro starts in chapter 26:7, where Job describes God's creative acts. God himself speaks audibly and puts to rest the evolution theories. The first question is, "Where were you when I laid earth's foundations and hung the planets in space?" Some loaded question. Now a more localized question: "Do you know how I put limits and boundaries on the seas?" In other words, what divides fresh and salt water? Then a broader question, "Can you control Kesil or Khima (the Pleiades and Orion)? Can you control the earth's rotation so the Southern Cross or Ursa Major and Minor happen in season?"

Job was obviously familiar with these constellations, as Nimrod was at Babel. Chapter 39 measures the seasons for birth and new life. Notice, God doesn't mess around with creepy-crawly bugs. He goes straight to intermediate animals. Here, God is not reprimanding Job for anything he did in error. As a matter of fact, God's purpose here seems to be to prevent Job from getting a swelled head.

God mentions the onager (wild ass), the ox, the ostrich, and the stork. He describes the ostrich as being a "birdbrain" and was created that way. But her speed puts horse and rider to shame.

Here is mentioned cavalry of the day, so Romans didn't ride to battle at first. Mentioned here is the hawk and eagle being guided in flight by unseen forces such as earth's magnetic forces.

God pauses for some sort of response. Job cannot give any sensible or logical response and asks God to continue. God encourages Job to be satisfied with what he has, then the fun part starts.

In chapter 40:15, God mentions animals that must be known at the time of Job, approximately 900 BC. The word *dinosaur* is a twentieth-century term. Biblical language uses the term *behemoth*. This term refers to any extraordinarily large animal, so it can include what we call dinosaurs, whales, giant squids, and possibly crocs.

Some are mentioned in more detail. Verses 15–18 describe herbivore, so this animal can't be a croc. He eats grass. His strength is in his hips and stomach. Ever seen pictures of a *Brontosaurus* or *Triceratops*? The description is *not* of any sea creature or other land animal. Dinosaurs lived, and museums are full of their bones. Here, God is describing two to Job, two thousand years after the flood. This means they came through the flood and survived. No meteor strike here, guys. Chapter 41 describes a leviathan (superbig sea creature). It cannot be caught on hook and line or harpooned. This describes *not* a large shark or a whale, because both these can be caught. This can only be describing a megalodon.

Chapter 41:12–16 describe a well-contoured animal that cannot be bridled or ridden. The problem is his large teeth. The animal has a coat of scales. This scaly covering cannot be pierced or parted, because the scales overlap and are joined. This is exactly what Wyrex, excavated in Montana in 2002, had—scales, not feathers. Which is correct, archeological finds or evolutionary guesses?

Here we have an accurate description of a *T. rex*, or king lizard, in the book of Job, approximately 1000 BC. *T. rex* having feathers is only an evolutionist's guess, another theory gone wrong. But we're not done. Chapter 41:19 gives a good description of a *Parasaurolophus*, or fire breather—possibly a dragon as in Rupert books? I prefer to believe the *Parasaurolophus* had the same ability to "breathe" or "spit" fire that the bombardier beetle has today. This beetle uses tiny amounts of hydroquinone and hydrogen peroxide in equal amounts. They are squirted from separate sacs in its abdomen. When the chemicals come together, they produce a small spark, thus discouraging predators. These same two chemicals were used in WWII torpedoes in larger amounts. This is also an enigma for evolutionists. How did this species, in varieties, ever develop without blowing their asses off? A little too much and they're up in smoke and food for predators, a little less and no predator gets scared off—dead either way.

Use your heads, guys. From 41:19 to the end of the chapter, this is a dinosaur, guys. It came through the flood and was contemporary with man up to about one thousand years ago. And don't tell any Brit that King George's dragon is a myth. The dinosaurs are all described as having power in their hips. This denotes they mostly, but not all, stood on two legs.

Job kept his wayward, malinformed friends, who, I'm sure, learned to trust God more from Job's ordeal. Job died at the age of 140 as a great-great-great-grandfather, even after starting a second family.

Notice here, just as a side note. Although Job seems (to me, at any rate) to be on an equal footing with God, he dies, and nothing indicates he was *not* taken to heaven in a whirlwind or any other.

CHAPTER 22

Psalms: Mostly Attributed to King David

MOST OF THE Psalms are written to give praise to a sovereign extraterrestrial. Little specific contact with extraterrestrial life forms is mentioned. Chapter 18 does, however, refer to God as savior, before the advent of Christ. God in human form appears in the New Testament. Curious. In 31:9, David does make a distinction between soul and body as being separate. In chapter 32:6–9, he gives credit to God for creation; 72:8–10 repeats that the descendants of Abraham would inherit Canaan.

David seeks God's help (in Psalm 83:1–9) in confounding the plans of the Edomites, Ishmaelites, Moabites, Amalekites, and Assyrians, in confounding their plans to wipe Israel from the face of the earth as they have promised to try and do. Sound familiar in today's headlines? These nations all serve idols (see Psalm 97:7).

Psalm 104:7–20 recounts the flood, not any meteor strikes, and 104:29 tells specifically that the spirit comes from God, as a specific and separate part of creation. It is a life force that God gives. In verse 29, specific mention is made that the soul and body return to the dust.

See again chapter 31:9. Again, this says that man is made in God's image, which is triune—body, soul, and spirit. Body (*soma*) is from the dust and returns there. Spirit (*nephesh*) is the life force from God and returns there immediately at death. Soul (psyche) is unique to man. It is his personality, and it ceases to be at death, it sleeps, and David, Solomon, Job, and Jesus (God, the extraterrestrial, incarnate says he will raise it along with the body when he returns.

See also chap 115:17. How much plainer can it be? Nobody goes to heaven at death, except the two already mentioned. Raising the souls or spirits of the dead is an impossibility for mediums or anyone else. Mediums contact demons, not dead ancestors. They're dead. Get it? *Dead.* In chapter 116:15, David says God remembrance of his "saints," not his communication with them in heaven or anywhere else.

I mention that David and others say that man is made in the image of God. This does not mean that man becomes a clone of God. God is Father, Son, and Holy Ghost (spirit). By contrast, man is body, soul, and spirit. Thus, the "image" parallel is made; God would never make a clone of himself.

So how do we know that Elohim is three, when the Shema says he is one? David calls God (Jehovah) his savior. But a savior does not come until Christ. So how does "God" show himself as three-in-one? See the following:

Jesus was born of a virgin (not a maiden or a young woman). He lived and was crucified under the governorship of Pilate (at least two stone columns have been excavated with Pilate's name on it). He was buried and rose on the third day. Please check any translation, Received or Alexandrian based, for the following verses.

The Holy Spirit raised Jesus from the dead (Romans 8:11). Jesus raised himself (in flesh and bones) (John 2:19). Everyone knows it was God who raised Jesus. Can you see the extraterrestrial connection yet?

Proverbs

Everyone needs good advice from time to time, some more than others. I'm sure that many, if they have gotten this far in this book, will immediately stop at this point. The wisdom of the wise is foolishness to those who choose to believe lies. If anyone should know the perils of adultery (chapter 4), Solomon should.

Some say that God is consummate love and cannot hate. Well, you're wrong. In chapter 6, Solomon says God hates

a proud look (arrogance),

any lie,

murderers,

false witness (backbiting),

a subverter of good deeds (e.g., goodwill charities profit only the owners),

anyone who plans evil (Hamas, Taliban, Muslim Brotherhood, etc.),

anyone who speaks evil where good is planned (e.g., Alexander the Coppersmith's opposition to Saint Paul), and

feet that run to evil (willful sinners).

So avoid these traps—this is the good advice of a wise man. In Zechariah chapter 5, we see two female angels delivering a basket (briefcase) to Nebuchadnezzar in Babylon. Solomon also refers (Proverbs chapter 11:1) to dishonest scales (weights and measures) as something to avoid like the plague. Chapter 12:1's bluntness is staggering. Anyone avoiding correction is stupid. Pride goes before destruction, and a haughty spirit before a fall.

Proverbs abounds with good, sound advice to anyone who will read and/or listen, but we are on a quest specifically for extraterrestrial activity in the Bible, so on we go.

Ecclesiastes is not really negative. It deals with realities. Chapter 2:16–20 tells it like it is.

Not many of us remember our grandparents, let alone WWI. All the surviving soldiers of WWI are dead. I only remember things my father and grandfather told me about.

Potions, oil of delay, incantations, etc., do not prevent death. What counts in the interim? Wealth, fame, possessions, friends, family? All must be left behind, and the writer tells it like it is. These realities are outlined in chapter 9, when the writer, like Job and David, says, "The living know they must die, but the dead know nothing." The dead have no say in what happens on earth when they are dead. Wills and testaments of the rich can be nullified by a good lawyer. Statues of pharaohs can and are defaced. Laws and statutes are changed to comply with the will of the living majority—even to the detriment of others. Such are the rulings of evil lawmakers, such as marriage (parades), stealing (Canadian senate), murder (US gun laws), and on and on.

The writer again repeats in chapter 12:7 that the body and psyche return to the ground and the spirit (alone) returns to God. I think someone is trying to make a point here. Ecclesiastes implores us to fear God and keep his commandments as being all that *really* is important, as God is and will be the one who has the last word.

The Song of Solomon could be misread as being unfit for minors. This is a mistake. What is here is a portrayal of the human condition and how best to handle it, but nothing extraterrestrial as such.

Isaiah tells of Immanuel to come, born of a virgin, not a maid or a young woman (chapter 7:10–16). This is the prophesied Jesus, Savior, spoken of by David. Many other prophecies are made about Immanuel. More than one hundred separate prophecies are fulfilled at Jesus's birth (someone counted them, I didn't). Truly this event is extraterrestrial. Do the math.

Chapter 14 recounts the fall of Lucifer and tells that Satan and his cohorts are excited (worried, concerned, troubled) at the prospect of Christ's coming. Even evil kings and mighty men who sleep in their graves cannot escape eventually seeing Jesus (verse 18–21). Certainly raising the dead is extraterrestrial. No?

Again in 26:19, the dead (all dead) dwell in the dust. This definitely implies that the grave is not permanent. Chapter 27:1 calls Satan a dragon, and even the power of the Pharaoh (chapter 30:2–3) cannot help the wicked. The saints (33:17) will behold God's glory. Chapter 37 repeats the Assyrian army's defeat by an angel (singular), where 175,000 are killed. By *one* angel? Some power.

Chapter 40:10 says God's (Jesus's) reward is with him. Not before his return and not before any pretrib rapture, as we'll see later. These old prophets knew what they were about and long before Tim LaHaye and his *Second Chance: Left Behind* gang.

There's more. From chapter 44 to 48, God, the extraterrestrial, does most of the speaking. With regard to creation, he says that he created everything suddenly—no long evolutionary millions of years. When I attended public school and high school in the '50s, the age of the earth according to evolution was ten to twenty million years old. Not long really. Today, the evolutionary age is two and a half billion years (give or take a few million). Give me a break! How did the earth age so fast? Possibly it will be some many billions more by the time my grandkids get out of university.

In chapter 51:13 and 16, God repeats that the earth was created by him and did not just happen by chance, and I ask again, what are the chances of an explosion in MacLean-Hunter or *Toronto Stars* offices of producing the next *Chatelaine* or tomorrow's late edition?

Isaiah ends by reminding us all that life continues at God's discretion.

Jeremiah is the faithful prophet contemporary with Zephaniah, Ezekiel, Habakkuk, Pharaoh Necho, and Pharaoh Hophrah.

It seems that Judah, Israel, is, through history, always in the middle, if not of the Hittites, Assyrians, Egyptians, Babylonians, Nubians, and goodness knows who else. And the Israelites still don't get God's message. Jeremiah tries (again) to get their attention, but idolatry seems to be rampant (still). In this period of the history, God, the extraterrestrial, is thoroughly frustrated with the continuing ignorance of the Israelites. It's as if they are collectively saying to God, "Choose someone else for a while."

Jeremiah persists through much gloom and doom. His writings are burned, and he is thrown into jail for his troubles and ends up being taken to Egypt. In Jeremiah 44:16–17, we see mention of the queen of heaven. In this case, it is Ishtar, a goddess of debauchery from Persia. The term *queen of heaven* is also applied to depraved women, goddesses, idols, and such under the guise of many different religions from many different countries. First was Semiramis from Babylon; also (in no particular order) are Isis, Ishtar, Diana, and so on to the present Mary, who has usurped God the Holy Spirit, as our advocate, giving advice to Jesus, no less.

Jeremiah prophesied approximately two hundred years before Alexander the Great came on the scene—not that long ago really.

Lamentations, attributed to Jeremiah, relates the suffering of a God-rejecting, sinful (willingly) nation. Jerusalem has been sacked (again), yet there are some within Israel that do not go along with the majority. Restoration is promised.

Ezekiel is a major prophet in Judaism and Hebrew writings. Ezekiel is also claimed as a prophet in Islam, even though Islam didn't come into existence for another 1,100 years. In Islam, Ezekiel and Zul-kifl are the same. The other idea is that they are *not* the same. In any case, the Hebrew and Christian view is that they are the same. Ezekiel has a unique "God" experience, so let's try to make sense of it.

In all, Ezekiel has seven visions (eyewitness accounts of extraterrestrial occurrences). First is that of Ezekiel sitting on the bank of a tributary of the Euphrates, the river (brook Chebar). His vision (eyewitness account) is that of God coming toward him. There is some speculation that Ezekiel had too much sun, or he was smoking wacky tobacky. This is not his nature; also he and other captives were resting. Resting usually takes place in the shade, especially in this part of the world. I can imagine some would be splashing in the river.

What comes toward them can best be described in twentieth-century language as an extravagant lunar rover, something like from a James Bond movie. Somehow, this one seems to have multiple "drivers" whose faces can be seen and their "dress" described as space suits. The fact that Ezekiel is with a crowd discounts the fact he might be having a fit, stroke, or out-of-body experience. This was not a "normal" angelic visit. When the vision moved, it did not turn in order to alter direction, but only altered direction by going there, something like a dancer learning the box step before learning the Arthur Murray turns. The appearance was that of being "alive." Another simile would be of a 1930s hay crib, with wheels, lightnings, and flashes emanating within the structure. It was multicolored with a rainbow hue in the middle.

This vision by Ezekiel and his friends really is unexplainable. I will not venture into science fiction, because anything of that sort is totally inadequate. An audible voice tells Ezekiel to prophesy to the captives still in Babylon. Jeremiah was prophesying to the Israelites that had returned to Israel months before, "Thus sayeth the Lord."

Ezekiel got the message right from the boss (the top). Before this is finished, Ezekiel is given a scroll to "eat" (digest), learn what to say and how to say it. This he does, and he gets the sensation of honey in his mouth. Then the being leaves with the sound of a huge flock of birds taking off and a "thunderous" noise (like a jet or rocket engine).

Ezekiel does as told and starts his first sermon by telling the Israelites that their righteousness (*salvation* in the New Testament) can be lost, and they must remain faithful to their first love, the Creator God.

Israel continues in sin. This is apparent, especially in chapter 8, when God shows Ezekiel what's going on in the temple. The Israelites had carved all kinds of statues, which they worshiped and gave obedience to. The pagan god Tammuz, a god of life, rebirth, and fertility, was worshiped in the temple. Tammuz's consort, Inanna, was the Babylonian equivalent of Ishtar, queen of heaven. The weeping was partly because the women were barren, partly because Tammuz was the supposed life for crops for the next year. It was a sad sight for Ezekiel.

The god Tammuz is revered by the followers of the Eastern Star and, ultimately, Freemasonry. It is directly linked in the third degree of Freemasonry as a ritual denoting life, death, and rebirth. Specifically, the rituals, God is showing Ezekiel, are an abomination. And he is to speak against it.

Eastern Star women perform the same rituals at the summer solstice. It's pagan, folks. What's your problem? My own conjecture here is that somehow, the ankh made an appearance here, the ankh being a symbol of life and rebirth.

It combines the male and female reproductive parts and is definitely appropriate for this to be one of the symbols, as described, being carved on the temple walls, along with other garbage that is *not* God's or condoned by him. This is only speculation, but if there is a better explanation, I'll hear it.

God ends speaking with Ezekiel and departs from the temple. The ark no longer has any purpose, except for Indiana Jones to retrieve it from the Nazis. LOL.

Again, the glory of the Lord appears to Ezekiel. This is obviously something visible, with an audible voice telling of another siege of Jerusalem. It seems God gets the pagan nations to do the punishing, but they still don't get the message.

In chapter 10, God is so fed up at this point. His presence leaves the temple, departs to the mountains, to the east of Jerusalem, for one "last" look, and then goes "up" to heaven. And it becomes inert. It is captured and remains for Indiana Jones to find it.

The description of God's presence in chapter 10 is the same as in chapter 1, no mistaking. Ezekiel still gets God's word through.

Israel and Judah continue idol worship, and another reference is made to a righteous man willingly sinning, that all the "good" he has done will come to naught (chapter 18:24).

Ezekiel continues to prophesy as God directed. A notable prophecy was the downfall of Egypt. This started to happen under Pharaoh Hophra, around 589 BCE.

Babylon, soon after, plunders Egypt. Chapter 32:6–8 describe an extraterrestrial event during the pillage of Egypt. Chapter 32 describes the sun and moon and stars as being "covered with a cloud." In 2009, excavations at the site of his capital Memphis give evidence of a great fire. Is this the "cloud" (smoke) predicted? The fire must have been similar to Nero burning Rome.

Chapter 37 is truly extraordinary. Some scholars call this a "literary expediency," and it does not seem possible this valley of dry bones can be other than symbolic of Israel being dead (totally depraved) as a nation for their continued rejection of

God. Ezekiel does say he was "in the spirit," an indication that God planted these scenes in his mind. In verses 11–14, this idea is expanded.

The miracle here of extraterrestrial import is not necessarily the vision, but the reality that Israel will become spiritually alive sometime in the future. God will "make it happen" and started the comeback in 1948 CE. This event is a vision. The graves literally opening (Matthew 27:52) is a real event. Ezekiel finally sees a vision of a restored "land" and the presence of God restored to the rebuilt city and temple.

Daniel

Lots of extraterrestrial stuff here. Daniel, better known as Daniel (not Belteshazzar), is Daniel. His three friends, Hananiah, Mishael, and Azariah, become better known as Shadrach, Meshach, and a bad Negro (Abednego). The last three have a trip to a blast furnace, courtesy of Nebuchadnezzar. They are extraterrestrially preserved by the angel of the Lord. Daniel survives a trip to the zoo (lion's den). Daniel also accurately predicts the king's dreams twice. Mysterious writing happens on a temple wall during a feast. Through these extraterrestrial happenings, both King Darius (6:245) and Nebuchadnezzar become believers in Daniel's God.

Daniel's visions have been debated. The vision of the four beasts is pretty well portrayed as being

lion = Babylon;
bear = Meds and Persians;
leopard = Greek;
fourth beast, with "iron teeth" = Rome.

What is extraordinary here is that all this is history, not tradition. What is even more extraordinary is that the Roman Empire is still happening today. Check your Internet. The Eastern Empire is not dead.

Alaric sacked the Western Empire in 410 CE. Constantine, in the East Empire, continues through the Byzantines to the modern age when we see the Crusades. In 790, Leo III smashed idols and icons, but they are back and worshiped by pagans worldwide.

The Byzantine Empire struggled on until the Renaissance, when many Byzantine scholars fled to Rome, where they continued their orthodox religion. Many, if not most, were Arians continuing in the footsteps of Origen, Eusebius, Jerome, etc.

Daniel's fourth beast continues today, continues through history, not tradition. Pope Benedict, quoting Palaiologos, second last Byzantine emperor, in a badly timed speech, berated Muslims for not being peace loving.

Apart from all this, the fourth beast lives in the Vatican today in "hiding." Daniel continues prophesying. In chapter 12:2–3, Daniel says the saints that are asleep in the dust shall rise. As we have seen from Solomon, Job, etc., this means their spirits that God received back will be reunited with their soul, and their flesh will return to their dry bones, as with Ezekiel's vision.

Daniel ends with God, the extraterrestrial, telling Daniel, he will sleep till the end, till Christ returns.

CHAPTER 23

S INCE THE BIBLE books do not follow in chronological order, Ezra relates a prophecy, at the beginning, to Jeremiah. Jeremiah comes soon. The Lord God of heaven is definitely a reference to Jehovah Elohim. Even Zoroastrianism was the main religion in Persia at the time. Zoroastrianism is monotheistic, but has idols, icons, and other statues depicting their god as a winged deity.

So the temple is rebuilt, but not without opposition, and Jerusalem also. Temple worship is resumed as it was under David.

Darius comes to the Persian throne through dubious means, but he is a "fair to good" administrator. He completes a canal at Suez and builds cities and roads, even into what is now modern Pakistan. He reduces tribute of oppressed nations, introduces universal coinage system, the Daric, and establishes a fair system of weights and measures.

I must jump ahead here to the book of Zechariah 5. This chapter gives an extraterrestrial account of two female angels (messenger types) heading to Persia to institute specifically this system. Did they visit Darius personally? We are not told. However, there are four notable "men of God" present in Persia at the time. It is entirely possible and very likely the female angels visited any one of them or all of them. In any case, it's history, not tradition, that Darius got the message and instituted these reforms. The prophets associated with Darius are Daniel,

Ezra, Haggai, Zechariah, and Nehemiah, so he got lots of good advice.

Darius's tomb looks similar to the famous Petra dwellings. Even with all God's men in the nation, the Judeans still don't get it. They intermarry with pagan women. Among the pagan countries mentioned is Egypt (chapter 9:2). At this time, the Egyptians have been steeped in fertility rites, as well as worship of Amun-Ra, the sun god, the same sun god that Constantine worshiped until his dying day. There is no Christian symbol on any of Constantine's coins. The first Christian king to have any symbol on his coins was Constantine's grandson. Even the Chi-Rho is a modified ankh, really a symbol of the sun god and ancient fertility religions.

Please research this area of tradition to satisfy yourselves that the ankh is in no way a Christian symbol, but a pagan symbol.

Ezra takes drastic measures and, at God's command, makes every illegitimate' marriage null and void.

Hosea

Hosea puts his finger on Israel's problem, in chapter 4:6, where he says it's Israel's responsibility to smarten up.

Joel

Joel agrees and predicts wonders in the heavens (2:30–31). (Notice the weather lately?)

Amos

Amos is a bit of an astronomer (as opposed to astrologer). Remember the Babel tower? We have Semiramis and family to thank for the introduction of the Zodiac. Semiramis wanted notoriety and proclaimed herself queen of heaven. Star clusters or formations were not named before Semiramis. The joining together of star formations was *her* idea to get famous. A whole religion grew up around the practice.

Today we call it astrology. It is a sham art and another method of worshiping creation. A person no more is influenced by the stars (planets) than my kitchen floor by the floor mop. When a person is born, he/she gets more influence from the attending nurses than all the stars in the galaxy. According to Amos, astrology is the "worship" of the stars and planets.

Obadiah

This minor prophet repeats Amos's warning (chapter 1:4). To set ones "nest" among the stars is very poetic but is only one of Israel's sins.

Jonah

The main story here with extraterrestrial significance is being called by God, running the other way, the final reconciliation, and the "big fish." Jonah also prophesies the destruction of Nineveh. God, the extraterrestrial, also causes a plant to grow fast and nearly suffocates Jonah.

Micah

Promise of the coming Messiah and the destruction of all idols.

Nahum

God's ability to destroy and renew. Destruction of Nineveh predicted, again also Thebes, in Egypt.

Habakkuk

The prophet's confirmation that the heavens and all that is in them were created by God and that he alone is the God of salvation.

Zephaniah

God's proclamation of his hatred of evil, foretelling of Christ's return (chapter 1:2–3), the destruction of astrologers and Freemasons (verse 5). Thus says the Lord.

Haggai

Basically a repeat of Zephaniah.

Zechariah

Zechariah prophesied during Darius's reign and probably contributed to his conversion. He has an angelic encounter (chapter 2:3). In chapter 4:1–2, he speaks verbally, while awake, to an angel. In chapter 5:1, he sees a flying carpet. In verse 5, he sees a female angel in a flying vehicle, then two female angels on a mission to Babylon, to correct their corrupt system of weights and measures. In chapter 6, here the prophet sees four chariots, 600 BC description of spacecraft driven or guided by angels.

Zechariah 11 prophesies against the followers of Masonry. The "right eye" here can only refer to a US one-dollar bill and those who worship money. Chapter 12:3 tells of the punishment of nations that war against Israel. Chapter 12:10 refers to the cross and refers specifically to God, since it is God speaking to the prophet. In chapter 14, the last part of verse 5 refers to the "holy ones" as the angels who did not rebel (not the dead in Christ) that comes soon after. Zechariah ends by reconfirming the return of Christ and the cessation of idol worship.

Malachi

Malachi repeats the message of Zechariah, the most important and earthshaking extraterrestrial event in history— the return of Christ. The Bible narrative of the Old Testament ends with the book of Malachi. The comment at the end of Malachi, in my Received Texts, says, "The end of the prophets." But history does not cease. There is a 395-year gap with no extraterrestrial activity, then Christ, the earthly extraterrestrial, comes on the scene.

I urge you to read for yourself. This does not mean history stopped. It just means that the Psalm 74:9 prophecy is fulfilled. In this time, there were *no* prophets or inspired writers. Instead, the Persians, Greeks, Syrians described in Isaiah 14 as a flying fiery dragon, Maccabees, and lastly the Romans have a lot to do in this period. We have the "little horn" that is Alexander, with his divided kingdom.

During this period, we see religious life in Israel develop. Also developed are the Pharisees, Sadducees, and Herodians and the institutions of Sanhedrin and synagogues and "lawyers" or scribes, as distinguished from the Old Testament "copiers" of the written texts. It is into this structured "mess'" that Christ, the Son (alter ego?) of God, the extraterrestrial, is born.

The New Testament is the story of God, the human extraterrestrial, and is full of much too much unexplained activity.